A HISTORY OF JEWISH MYSTICISM

ERNST MÜLLER

BARNES
&NOBLE
BOOKS
NEW YORK

Originally published in 1946.

This edition published by Barnes & Noble, Inc.

1995 Barnes & Noble Books

ISBN 1-56619-980-8

Printed and bound in the United States of America.
M 9 8 7 6 5 4 3 2 1

CONTENTS

PREFACE

THE object of this work is to give a comprehensive survey of the history of Jewish mysticism—one which shall cover the whole field and not only that part commonly known as Cabbalah. It also includes the contacts of Jewish with non-Jewish mysticism. While other works deal with various aspects of the subject in far greater detail, this work aims particularly at placing in their proper perspective the mystical spirit of the Bible itself, the mystical tendencies in the apocalyptic literature and the allegorical exegesis of the Bible, and the existence of an ancient esoteric lore closely connected with the popular Agada. In his treatment of the Zohar the author has proceeded on the lines of the Introduction and the translations which he has already published. The later epochs of the Cabbalah he has only been able to treat somewhat cursorily, partly because war conditions prevented him from having access to the most important sources. In view of the numerous modern works dealing with Chassidism it was not necessary to refer to more than the most essential points in this movement. The last chapter touches briefly on non-Jewish movements akin to the Cabbalah.

The notes contain much historical and other information supplementary to the text, while the Appendix fills out the picture given in the text by a selection of passages from the original works which speak for themselves.

The work was written originally in German. It has been translated into English by Mr. Maurice Simon, the well-known scholar and translator of the Midrash and Zohar. But Mr. Simon's participation in the book, for which I cannot sufficiently thank him, goes far beyond that of a mere translator, particularly in the fact that his intimate knowledge of the subject has enabled him to treat the difficult material in a proper style. In fact, the final form of the text may be regarded as a joint production.

I am also deeply grateful to my dear wife Freda Müller, whose encouragement and sympathy have been invaluable to me at every stage of the work, and who has also given me great assistance on the technical side.

E. M.

The quotations from the Talmud, Midrash, and Zohar (when not otherwise stated) are taken by kind permission from the translations of these works published by the Soncino Press.

The Philo quotations are taken partly by kind permission from *The Loeb Classical Library* published in London by William Heinemann Ltd., in the translation by F. H. Colson, M.A., and the Rev. G. H. Whitaker, M.A.

INTRODUCTION

JEWISH mysticism is that form of the Jewish religion which, like the mysticisms of other religions, seeks especially to cultivate personal communion between the worshipper and God. This communion is of course an essential feature of the ordinary talmudical Judaism also. But whereas in talmudical Judaism it is subsidiary to the observance of the precepts, and to some extent an offshoot of it, in mysticism it takes the first place and can itself become the source of religious practice and observance. Hence the distinguishing mark of mysticism in Judaism as in other religions is a peculiar intensity of religious feeling, rising frequently to ecstasy, which gives to it a dynamic force unknown to the ordinary religion.

Jewish mysticism has both a devotional or practical and an intellectual or speculative side. On its devotional side it emphasises those aspects of the precepts which serve to promote direct communion between the worshipper and God, and in consequence it attaches a particular importance to prayer. On its speculative side it is especially concerned with outlining and bringing into relief the link or links between God and man, or more generally between the Creator and the universe. On this side therefore it has close affinities with the Jewish religious philosophy of the Middle Ages, which also inquires primarily into the relation between God and the universe. But it differs entirely from this inquiry in its method of approach to the main problem, and consequently in all of its subsidiary themes. Whereas religious philosophy is essentially logical, proceeding from the known to the unknown, mysticism is essentially intuitional, visualising the unknown by means of some inner insight granted only to the " mystic " or initiated, and working down from that to the known. Certainly its intuition is not able any more than the philosophical logic to realise completely the true nature of God. But unlike philosophy it has not to content itself with purely negative results, and it is able to body forth a whole world of beings intermediate between man and God, or between the world and God, and forming a link or links between them, from angels only little removed from man to Sefiroth barely distinguishable from God.

With these intermediate beings Jewish mysticism claims a peculiar and intimate acquaintance, and it is this feature which chiefly distinguishes it, as a doctrine, from *talmud torah* proper on the one hand and from religious philosophy on the other, while it gives to it a certain affinity with the Agadic Midrash, as pointed out in ch. II of this work. The actual doctrine is worked out on three lines which may be called respectively the theological, the psychological, and the ethical. On the theological side the object is to specify the beings intermediate between God and man and arrange them in grades and hierarchies according to their possession of creative powers or other divine qualities. On the psychological side the object is to show man how to develop the intuitional faculty, called the *neshamah* or super-soul, which enables him to apprehend these beings and place himself in communion with them, and through them with God. Finally on the ethical side it teaches how this communion can be applied to human life and conduct. These three heads embrace practically the whole of Jewish mystical doctrine, the historical development of which will be traced in the following pages.

In that development we can distinguish more or less clearly four epochs :—

(1). The biblical period. In connection with this we can hardly speak of mystical theories, but the whole religious life is in it more deeply penetrated than in later epochs with what may be called the mystical consciousness.

(2). The period of the old Jewish esoteric teaching, in which mystical theories are still in a crude state, but embrace nearly all sides of the religious life.

(3). The period of the Cabbalah proper, characterised by systematic presentations of the mystical doctrine as a whole, together with special treatment of particular features.

(4). The period of Chassidism, which out of the mystical teaching developed a new style of religious feeling and conduct.

I

MYSTICAL ASPECTS OF THE BIBLE

ACCORDING to the Cabbalists, most portions of the Bible contain, besides the literal meaning, a deeper underlying meaning, by means of which the initiated can attain to a closer communion with the Deity. However this may be, there is no question that the Old Testament contains doctrines, ideas, and expressions, of what may be called a mystical import, that is to say, which even taken at their face value aim deliberately at setting the mind on a mystical train of thought and which derive their chief or even their only significance from their mystical implications. This mystical element in the Old Testament varies somewhat in character in the three sections into which the Hebrew Scriptures are divided by the Massorah—the Torah, containing the Pentateuch, the Nebiim or prophets, containing besides the prophetic writings proper the earlier historical works—Joshua, Judges, Samuel, and Kings[1]—and the Hagiographa, or Sacred Writings, containing the rest, viz., Psalms, Proverbs, Job, the Five Scrolls, Daniel, Ezra, Nehemiah, and Chronicles. The mystical element of the Old Testament is best considered in each of these sections separately, though for this purpose it is advisable to include the Book of Daniel with the prophets, and not in the Hagiographa.

1. THE TORAH

The Torah is the text-book of the cult of ancient Israel, containing the regulations for its religious life and worship. The ritual which it prescribes is found when dispassionately examined to be neither purely formalistic, without any inner meaning, nor purely symbolical, deriving its meaning only from certain spiritual ideas which it adumbrates. This ritual possessed a certain magic potency which made it a living force in the life of its practitioners, fixing as it did their attention on some transcendental force as their source of life and guidance. This has been conclusively proved by Oskar Goldberg in his book *Die Wirklichkeit der Hebräer*, though Goldberg overrates the importance of the magic element as against the religious and spiritual.

According to the biblical account, the introduction of the Mosaic code was accompanied in all its phases by miracles of a kind which pointed to a genuine connection between external nature and a supra-sensual world. Thus in the fire of the burning bush Moses experiences for the first time his meeting with the Godhead, and in fire and lightning on Mount Sinai the religion of Israel, both as creed and law, is founded.

The Mosaic religious system had its local centre in the Sanctuary of the Wilderness, called "Tent of Meeting", the movable prototype of the subsequent Temple ; its chief outward manifestation in the sacrifices ; its periodical rhythm in the celebration of the festivals ; and its human ministrants in the Priesthood. All four of these elements had their mystical aspect. The dimensions and proportions of the Sanctuary[2] and the prescriptions regarding the holy vessels and their materials were meant to represent certain features observable in the order of the universe, as did also no doubt the Egyptian pyramids, though in a different way. In Philo of Alexandria[3] and in Josephus Flavius[4] we find symbolical explanations which cannot have been invented by them and which are probably connected for the most part with ancient traditions. Thus they tell us that the three divisions of the Sanctuary correspond to the three divisions of the universe: heaven, sea, and land[5] ; the four fabrics which were used in the sacred tent and in the priestly garments to the four elements ; the seven branches of the holy candlestick to the seven planets ; the twelve loaves of the shewbread, as also the twelve precious stones on the breastplate of the High Priest, to the twelve signs of the zodiac and their earthly counterpart, the twelve tribes of Israel.

The sacrifices were divided into blood-offerings and bloodless offerings. In the sprinkling of the blood and the burning on the altar, which took place with the former, there was effected an intimate union of blood and fire which expressed complete self-sacrifice on the part of the human being to the Power which guides the world. The latter again signify the extraction from the earth of its vegetative sustenance, whilst the incense is an offering of that material substance which has most affinity with the spiritual.

The festivals also, which are partly nature and partly national celebrations, have a directly religious character, in virtue of which they are in general designated as " sabbaths ". By means of the sacrifices prescribed for them they so to speak harness the strivings for a higher life to the rhythm of the revolving year, with which also the bringing of the firstfruits is connected. The weekly recurring Sabbath is the most typical and, along with the Day of Atonement, the holiest day in the Jewish calendar. The Day of Atonement itself is in virtue of the general forgiveness which it brings, of the striking ceremony of the two he-goats, of the prescribed fast, and of the proclamation of the Name of God in the Holy of Holies, a day of most intimate union with God for the whole people.

It goes without saying that the priesthood, and especially the office of the High Priest, have more than a merely ritualistic significance. Certainly in the ancient Israelitish cult the priests did not occupy the same dominating position, as masters of magic and mystery, as in the Egyptian and other ancient heathen religions. Perhaps also they were to a lesser extent regarded as initiated, and more as sinful human beings who owed their office simply to their membership of the priestly tribe of Levi and the family of Aaron, combined with their solemn anointment. All the same their position within the cult as a whole and particularly in the sacrificial service cannot be understood without presuming a mystical background, with which of course was connected the noble social idea that they were to set an example to the people itself chosen to be " holy, a people of priests ".

In all the religious ceremonies of the Mosaic cult the High Priest is as intermediary the representative of the people before God, and equally the representative of God to the people. This appears above all in the fact that in the sacrifice he performs the central ceremony of sprinkling, which was carried out for the first time by Moses on his descent from Mount Sinai (Ex. XXIV, 6), as an act which could be regarded as particularly suited to effect a covenant between God and Israel.[6]

Two functions of the High Priest bring out with special force the mystical side of his office : the priestly blessing, with which went the utterance of the otherwise unpronounceable Divine Name, and the oracle of the Urim and Tummim which was carried on the breast of the High Priest, and the exact method of using which is not indicated in the biblical text.

This utterance of the Divine Name was undoubtedly intended to form some kind of link between God and the worshipper, in virtue of some special, mystical potency ascribed to that Name, as distinguished from the other names of God. For we must carefully bear in mind that the plethora of the divine names in the bible is no meaningless tautology. The theory of modern biblical criticism, that the constant recurrence of the two names Jehovah and Elohim provides a basis for dissecting the bible into a number of sources which have passed through various redactions, will not bear examination. For on this assumption we can attach no meaning to the solemn identification of the two in Deuteronomy IV, 35, 39, "Jehovah, He is Elohim" (more correctly, "the Elohim"), and again in 1 Kings, XVIII, 39, where this proclamation is even more impressive, being made by the whole people.[7] As was pointed out more than a hundred years ago by M. H. Landauer in his penetrating studies on the Pentateuch, a radical distinction can be observed in the use of the two names. This appears for one thing in the plural form of the name Elohim, for another thing in the fact that this name is used not only for the God of Israel, but also for divine powers in general (even, for example, the apparition of Samuel conjured up by Saul from the grave).[8] Landauer shows also how the various other designations of the God-head are deliberately and methodically used, especially in the story of Abraham, to denote various traits and activities of the Divine Being. The name of the " Self-existent ", which was still hidden from the Patriarchs, was for the first time communicated to Moses in the vision of the burning bush in the form " Ehyeh asher Ehyeh ".

It is further to be noted that in the whole biblical terminology the " Name of YHWH " is distinguished from YHWH himself. It is not to be understood as a mere substitute for YHWH, as is held by Grether in his otherwise excellent work " Name und Wort Gottes ". Throughout the Scriptures, from the record of the first worship of God in the days of Enosh (Gen. IV, 26), we find the expression " to call on the name of God ", implying that only the name of the Godhead is accessible to human appeal, not its fundamental essence. The " Tent of Meeting ", the Temple, and likewise the altars used in primitive worship[9], as also the Ark of the Covenant (vide e.g. 2 Sam. VI, 2), are places where not the Godhead itself but its " Name " abides. The sacredness of the name of God is further indicated in the third of the Ten Commandments which forbids its misuse. The priestly blessing was meant to cause the name of God to rest on the Children of Israel.[10] The accounts in Philo and the Talmud of the awe-inspiring occurrences which followed the utterance by the High Priest of the hidden Name in the Holy of Holies on the Day of Atonement must, even where fabulous, have been founded on fact.

Thus with the names in general a line must have been drawn between the unattainable divine essence and its revealed forms which can be grasped by human beings who are properly prepared for the task. This limitation, which is valid even for the men who are nearest to God, is described most pregnantly in the account in Exodus XXXIII, 17, sqq., where Moses asks to see the Godhead, but is able to behold only its " back ", not its " countenance ".

Apart from God, other superhuman beings appear constantly in the biblical narrative from its very beginning, as for instance the Cherubim at the entrance of Paradise (Gen. III, 24), the " sons of God " who ally themselves with the daughters of men (*Ib.* VI, 2), and above all the angels in the stories of the Patriarchs—the " angel of YHWH " who met Hagar, the three angels who visited Abraham, those who appeared to Jacob in his dream, and the one with whom he fought and who had in the end to bless him. The " angel of YHWH " reveals himself to Moses in the thornbush, and it is the same being who at first accompanies Moses to the holy tent and who leads the people of Israel through the wilderness. This one must be regarded as the guardian angel of the people of Israel of whom we read in Ex. XXIII, 20 and 21 : " Behold I send an angel before thee, to keep thee in the way and to bring thee into the place which I have prepared. Beware of him and obey his voice ; provoke him not, for he will not pardon your transgressions ; for My name is in him." Benamozegh justly points out that this angel—who in Jewish tradition is sometimes identified with the archangel Michael—has the same significance for Israel as for the other peoples was assigned by the Talmud to the so-called " Sarim " (princes)[11] ; and these too are mentioned by the Septuagint in a remarkable rendering of Deut. XXXII, 8. The stars also appear occasionally as living beings, e.g. in Job XXXVIII, 7, where the " morning stars " are mentioned along with the " sons of God ".

Apart from angels, other terms of a more abstract character are used in the Bible to indicate substances intermediate between God and the world. These terms, with which great play was made in later Jewish thought, are by no means to be understood even in their original setting as having been used in a poetic or allegorical sense. They are to be regarded as designating actually existing divine beings, and not as abstract qualities or faculties, or as artificial personifications, as supposed by Castelli in his study on biblical and talmudical mysticism.

Foremost among these terms is that of *Kabod*. In Jewish and Christian theology this term is incorrectly taken as meaning " honour " or " glory ". As Goldberg has pointed out, however, it is connected etymologically with the adjective *kabed*, " heavy ", and designates a primary materialisation of the divine essence, a " condensation into a cloud ".[12] This is also hinted in the Greek translation, $\delta\delta\xi\alpha$ = appearance. Thus it is the " Kabod of YHWH " which rests on Mount Sinai, and which Moses also desires to behold (Ex. XXXIII, 18).

The term *Shechinah*, which plays such a central part in the system of Chassidism, does not itself occur in the Bible, but etymologically it is of biblical origin. It applies to the " abiding " (*Inwohnung*) of God in the world (Buber), and particularly to the resting of His manifestation on Mount Sinai and in the holy precinct of the Mishcan.

In the passage describing God's revelation to Moses in Ex. XXXIII, 17 *sqq.*, the term *makom*, place or space, is used to indicate the all-pervading presence of the Godhead, and on this account it was made in talmudical times into a separate name of God.[13]

Rather more concrete, it would appear, is the " spirit " or " breath " of God (*Ruach Elohim*) which appears in the story of the creation, as setting in motion the first development in the primeval chaos. As a higher principle it is the spirit which pervades the world, which, e.g., according to Joel III, 1, God pours over all flesh, and which in Ps. LI, 13, is designated the " holy spirit " working in the human soul. Here may also be mentioned the " face of God ", an expression by which the presence of God is always directly or indirectly signified.

The concept of " Wisdom " also, as personified in ch. VIII and IX of the Book of Proverbs, was in subsequent interpretations brought into connection with the personified Sophia of the pre-Christian and early Christian Gnosis (*v.* p. 28)

Perhaps the most important passages in the Bible bearing on this subject are those which speak of the " Word of

God ". As the angel was the intermediary between God and man for the sense of sight, so the "word" was the intermediary for the sense of hearing ; and the prophets on their side never spoke out of their own wisdom, but only because the "Word of God" came to them or the "Mouth of God" spoke through them (e.g., Is. XL, 5). Nay more, the words "And God said, Let there be light" have been interpreted from the earliest times to indicate the Word of God as the real creative power. The Targum of Onkelos in its rendering of the first chapter of Genesis even designates the Creator as the "Word" (*memra*). This rendering belongs to a time when the concept of the Logos, which had its forerunners in the oldest Greek philosophy (e.g., in Heraclitus), reached its full development in Philo of Alexandria and so inspired the opening sentence of the Gospel of Saint John, "In the beginning was the Word".[14]

2. PROPHECY

The nature of prophecy, as presented to us in the prophetical works of the Bible, cannot be explained without the assumption of a mystical background consisting in a direct communication with God. Certainly the prophetic utterances are not all of one stamp, and one would not say this of all of them. Their ethical force and incisiveness, their social idealism, their clear-cut monotheism might be attributed to the workings of the rational faculties pure and simple ; even their awe-inspiring predictions of the downfall of the two Israelitish kingdoms, as also of the fate in store for the nations, large and small, which surrounded Israel, could be traced back to a highly developed political insight. But the claim of the prophets to be guided by higher powers is bound up in many cases with the very manner of their first call to prophecy, it expresses itself in the very form of their utterances, which is not so much poetical as ecstatic, corresponding to the experience which produced it. This claim is also in line with the absolute certainty with which they made their predictions. In two points the prophetic utterance rises to heights which cannot at all be comprehended rationalistically, in the apocalyptic or messianic vision of distant times (Isaiah, Joel, Zephaniah, Zechariah, Malachi, Daniel), where the natural course of history fuses into the fulfilment of divine purposes, and in the supra-sensual revelations of the Godhead (Isaiah, Ezekiel, Daniel).

In the prophet Elijah the Bible presents us with a figure which intervenes in the religious history of Israel like a superhuman being (e.g., in the struggle with the priests of Baal), sweeping over the land like a hurricane until it is carried to heaven by fiery steeds. In later times this prophetic figure, whose return was proclaimed by Malachi, the last of the prophets, as heralding the Messiah, was honoured by Jews and Christians alike, though in different ways, as a heavenly guide who was always near and frequently appeared on earth and in human form.

In addition to the numerous individual messengers of God whose visions and announcements are recorded in the Scriptures, we find mention in the Bible of " sons " (i.e. disciples) " of the prophets ". These constituted the oldest corporate body (outside of the priesthood) known to us in Judaism. Its aim was to arouse the higher faculties of the soul—in this case that of prophecy—through the medium of ecstasy. Thus we read in the tenth chapter of the first book of Samuel how Saul after his first meeting with Samuel attached himself to such a group of wandering *Nebiim*, whose divine ecstasy and power of prophecy he immediately imbibed.

There were also in biblical times other corporate bodies with a particular religious tendency containing perhaps the germ of those sects in which in later times a mystical tradition was preserved and developed. Such were the Nazirites, whose origin is recorded in the sixth chapter of Numbers, and who were distinguished by a strict vow of ritual purity. The Rechabites, of whom we read in Jeremiah XXXV, 2, formed a religious brotherhood which may possibly have had a mystical trend, and the same may be said of the Kenites mentioned in connection with them in 1 Chron.,

II, 55, and the "Sons of Korah" to whom many of the Psalms are attributed.

3. HAGIOGRAPHA

The Book of Psalms is a many-sided work which reflects every aspect of the religious mind—its delight in religious practice and worship, its awe-struck wonder at God's creative power as revealed in Nature, its hopes for a Messianic redemption of the Jewish people, its vision of the ultimate reward of the righteous, above all its striving to shape for the soul a new inner life through the power of faith. But beyond and above all this the Psalms sometimes penetrate into a mystical realm which is the very fountain-head of piety and morality, as has always been recognised by those whose minds are attuned to such revelations.[15] So while the Book of Psalms has been the most important single work of the Bible for the religious life of both Jews and Christians, it has also served as a book of mystical secrets, even of magical potency, which can be used in cases of sickness and death for the healing of body and soul, and also for purposes of inner self-communion. There does in fact exist a "Sefer Shimmush Tehillim", a Book for the (mystical) use of the Psalms, while various scholars noted for their piety have been credited with the power of working wonders by means of the Psalms.[16]

A few instances may be adduced of Psalms in which a mystical element appears not in the recondite sense assigned by later interpretation, but in the simple and literal meaning. Psalm XVIII in powerful and simple language portrays God coming to the rescue of King David in earthquake, storm, and tempest; Psalm XXIX describes how the "voice of God" thunders through Nature with terrifying effect. A gentler note is struck in Psalm XIX, of which the first part sounds almost like a hymn to the sun, and which then depicts the same divine power mirroring itself in the soul which follows God's teaching.

A new basis is found for piety in the longing of the isolated soul not only, as in Psalms XLII and XLIII, for the religious service in the Temple, but also, as in Psalm XXIII, for the " Shepherd who causes her to lie down in green meadows " and is with her even in the valley of the shadow of death. Especially mysterious is the power of " the soul which dwells in the shadow of the Highest ", which in Psalm XCI is pictured as being borne on the wings of angels and treading fearlessly and harmlessly on adders and lions. Already in Talmudic times this Psalm was interpreted as referring to the soul nestling in God after death, and by mystics it was applied to kindred inner experiences also. In the Midrash and Zohar it is designated " Song of Afflictions " (*Shir shel Pega 'im*), and it is included in the service for the dead.

The most intimate portions of the Psalms deal with the individual man, and Psalm CXXXIX pictures the ubiquity of God as instanced both in the body and the soul of man, referring enigmatically to his origin as a being moulded from the depths of the earth. Concurrently it expresses the wish that God may examine man completely and know his heart, in order so " to guide him in the way of eternity ". Ever and anon we are shown the gulf which the hopeful or despairing soul has to bridge, as in the pregnant words of the fifth verse of Psalm CXVIII, " out of my straits I called upon the Lord, He answered me from the expanse." A piety speaking from the deepest experience of the individual soul and finding only therein its consummation is revealed most clearly in the words of Psalm LI : " Hide Thy face from my sins and blot out all my iniquities. Create in me a clean heart, O God, and renew a steadfast spirit within me. Cast me not away from Thy presence, and take not Thy holy spirit from me " (vv. 11–13). And a still more intimate communion is besought in the words of Psalm LXXXVI, 11 : "Teach me, O Lord, Thy way, that I may walk in Thy truth, make one[17] my heart to fear Thy name."

The 119th Psalm has a connection with mysticism of quite a different character. This Psalm contains 176 verses and is arranged in an eightfold alphabetical acrostic, that is to say, each successive eight verses commence with the same letter of the alphabet. It is more than probable—as seems to have been already surmised by the Church Father Jerome[18]—that there is some relation between the contents of each eight-verse strophe and the supposed character of the letter with which it begins. Such an idea would be fantastic, were it not that we have good grounds for locating in the Bible the root of an important element of the subsequent Cabbalah, namely, the mysticism of sounds and letters.

On this supposition the deep reverence paid to the name of God is given a linguistic basis in the fact that the sounds of which that name is composed are specially distinguished in regard both to their character and their place in the alphabet. While the Hebrew alphabet consists nominally of consonants only, the breathing-sounds constitute in a certain way a middle stage between consonants and vowels, and certainly occupy a rank superior to that of the other consonants. It is from these breathing-sounds that the two principal divine names are made up, viz. EHYH (*vide* Exodus III, 14), and the one regularly used, YHWH. What is more, the four letters out of which both names are made up are symmetrically arranged within the first ten letters of the alphabet, occupying the first place, the fifth, the sixth, and the tenth. This correspondence of letter and number is of the same kind as in the Cabbalistic " Gematria " (*v.* p. 49 *infra*). If further the numerical values of the four letters are added together, the result is 26, a number closely related to the numerical values of a great many other words of religious-historical significance. Considerations of this kind no doubt played their part in the transformation of Hebrew into a sacred language—not but what the Hebrew of the Bible is in its very structure of a much more elevated character than the other kindred Semitic languages and the later spoken and written Aramaic and Rabbinic Hebrew. The Hebrew square character, which is nowhere found in inscriptions, seems also to have been a sacred script.[19]

Another indication that certain methods akin to letter-mysticism, namely, artificial alphabets, were already known in biblical times is provided by the employment in the book of Jeremiah (ch. LI) of an alphabet of this kind, in which the last letter of the ordinary alphabet is substituted for the first, the last but one for the second, and so forth. Thus ב becomes ש and ל becomes ך.

We have said nothing so far of the two most important mystical passages in the Bible—the account of the creation in Genesis and the description of the Divine Throne in Ezekiel. These two subjects form the central themes of the later mystical doctrine, in connection with which they will therefore be considered.

NOTES TO CHAPTER I

[1] From the point of view of mysticism, these are more akin to the Torah than to the Prophets.

[2] These correspond throughout to musical harmonics, and from the occultist point of view also to proportions of the human organism. On examination the scheme of the double square is found to be predominant. The Holy of Holies had the form of a cube, a fact to which attention is called in 1 Kings, VI, 20. In the New Testament also (Rev. XXI, 16) the " New Jerusalem " is described in the form of a cube.

[3] In " De Specialibus Legibus " and elsewhere.

[4] In the " Antiquities ", Book III, ch. 4–6.

[5] B. Jacob in his book " Der Pentateuch " sees in the double expression " Holy of Holies " a reflection of the expression " Heaven of Heavens " used to designate the highest or inmost heaven. For the symbolism of the Tent of Meeting in detail see also Bähr, " Symbolik des mosaischen Kultus ", and M. H. Landauer, " Wesen und Form des Pentateuchs ".

[6] This is also emphasised by Abelson in his book " Jewish Mysticism ". Cf. also Martin Buber, " Königtum Gottes ", 139 sqq.

[7] So too Ps. CXLIV, 15, praises Israel as the people " whose God is YHWH ".

[8] So too in Ex. IV, 16, Moses as Aaron's inspirer is called " Elohim ".

[9] V. for instance Ex. XX, 24, where it says " In all places where I record My name I will come to thee and I will bless thee."

[10] V. Numbers, VI, 22–27.

[11] " Israel et l'Humanité ", ch. IX, " L'Idée des Sarim ou Anges Guardiens."

[12] V. O. Goldberg, " Die Wirklichkeit der Hebräer," pp. 65 and 104.

[13] V. p. 33.

[14] Grether points out that in 225 out of 234 places in the Bible where the expression *dabar* is used, it denotes a word of God either derived from a prophet or proclaimed by one, while in the remaining places it mostly denotes a " legal revelation ".

[15] For the influence of the Psalms through the ages v. Prothero, " The Psalms in Human Life ". Outside of Judaism, the mystical side of the Psalms has been emphasised in the ancient Gnostic work " Pistis Sophia," and in recent times by among others the celebrated mystic Immanuel Swedenborg.

[16] *Cf.* the Yiddish novel of Shalom Ash, " Der Tillimsoger ", which is supposed to be based on the life of the chassidic " Zaddik " Yehiel of Zloczow.

[17] The idea of the unity of the heart in the Psalms has been particularly dwelt upon in recent times by Hermann Cohen.

[18] Especially in a " Letter to Marcella ".

[19] It is known in Jewish tradition as the " Assyrian script ", the assumption being that it was brought back by the Jews from the Babylonian exile. This may perhaps indicate that, at the time when the foundations were being laid for a specific Jewish secret doctrine (*v.* ch. IV), this script was brought into use in order to preserve the biblical text in a worthy form for later times when it was obvious that Hebrew would cease to function as a language of daily intercourse.

II

AGADA, ALLEGORY, AND APOCALYPSE

TOWARDS the end of the biblical period and in the period immediately following, the mystical element in Jewish literature was developed more consciously and intensively, though it did not yet reach the stage of specific Jewish secret doctrine. We have now to deal with three movements of thought which, though at first sight widely different from each other, are, nevertheless, both historically and in virtue of their content, all connected more or less closely with the beginnings of a Jewish mystical doctrine properly so-called. The first is to be found in the wide field of the midrashic and talmudic Agada[1]; the second in the allegorical exegesis of the Bible, especially that of Philo of Alexandria, along with kindred traces in the oldest translations of the Bible ; the third in the apocalyptic writings and fragments which have been preserved partly in Hebrew, partly in the Greek, Syriac and Old Slavonic languages.

1. MIDRASH AND AGADA

Midrash and Agada are store-houses of popular legend but they strike a deeper note. They body forth a world of imagination—aptly termed by Martin Buber "legend-bible" (Sagen-Bibel)—which contains also mystical visions, experiences, and ideas, presented in a popular form, and often appearing in the most unexpected places. The connection between Midrash and mysticism as a whole has not yet been systematically worked out ; but without doubt there is between them in many respects a close relationship, often amounting to identity, as is shown by the fact that the Zohar not only has incorporated several passages from the Talmud and Midrash, but is itself designated "Midrash of R. Simeon b. Yochai ". The name Midrash as such denotes only bible exegesis, of whatever kind,[2] and it is consequently difficult to determine in many cases the border-line

between agadic and mystical passages, or to decide whether
a particular book should be assigned to one class or
the other.   Apart from mystical passages in such
agadic works as the Midrash Rabba and Tanchuma, there
are many writings in the collection of old Midrashim
published by Adolf Jellinek under the title of "Beth
Ha-Midrash"[3] which belong throughout to the older
mystical literature.

The mystical Midrash employs the same methods of
biblical interpretation as the agadic.   One is to link together
biblical verses which seem to have no connection with each
other but contain the same word or expression.   Thus the
idea—based on the almost divine honour paid to wisdom[4]—
that the world was created through the agency of Wisdom
is supported by the fact that the Book of Genesis opens
with the words " In the beginning God created the heaven
and the earth," while in Psalm CXI the words ראשית
("beginning") and חכמה ("wisdom") are found in juxta-
position, so that it is possible to regard the word "beginning"
as being equivalent to " wisdom ".   One Aramaic translation
actually renders " With Wisdom God created . . ."   Often
again the more recondite interpretation was based on unusual
grammatical forms or even something abnormal in the script.
Thus when the word בהבראם ("when they were created")
in Genesis II, 4, was by a transposition of letters turned
into באברהם ("for Abraham")—implying that the world was
created for the sake of Abraham—this was justified by the
fact that the ה in the massoretic text is written small, as
though to indicate that there was something more there
than met the eye.   Again, the fact that the word וייצר
(and He formed) in verse 7 of the same chapter is
written with two yods is taken as an indication that
God created man with two inclinations, the good and
the evil (the word yezer signifying also "urge" or "inclination").

There are several striking midrashim and agadas which
deal with the story of the Creation from a mystical point
of view, and these seem to provide a more popular version

of the esoteric doctrine which was taught to the initiated under the title of " maaseh bereshith " (v. next chapter). Some characteristic passages may be quoted :

" And God said, Let there be light . . . R. Simeon b. R. Jehozadak asked R. Samuel b. Nahman : ' As I have heard that you are a master of haggadah, tell me whence the light was created.' He replied : ' The Holy One, blessed be He, wrapped Himself therein as in a robe and irradiated with the lustre of His majesty the whole world from one end to the other.' Now he had answered him in a whisper, whereupon he observed, ' There is a verse which states it explicitly : *Who coverest Thyself with light as with a garment* (Psalm CIV, 2), yet you say it in a whisper.'[5] ' Just as I heard it in a whisper, so have I told it to you in a whisper, he rejoined " (Bereshith Rabba III, 4).

Another saying speaks of the " primordial light " which was created long before the light of the sun, bringing it into close relationship with man, who was still a spiritual being at the time of the creation, and who will be such again at his consummation at the end of days. The passage runs as follows : " . . . For R. Eleazar said : The light which the Holy One, blessed be He, created on the first day, one could see thereby from one end of the world to the other ; but as soon as the Holy One, blessed be He, beheld the Generation of the Flood and the Generation of the Dispersion (v. Genesis XI, 9), and saw that their actions were corrupt, He arose and hid it from them, for it is said, *But from the wicked their light is withholden* (Job XXXVIII, 15). And for whom did He reserve it ? For the righteous in the time to come (i.e., the Messianic era, v. Aboth, II, 16), for it said, *And God saw the light that it was good* (Genesis, I, 4), and " good " means only the righteous, for it is said, *Say ye of the righteous that he is good* (Isaiah III, 10). As soon as He saw the light that He had reserved for the righteous, *He rejoiced at the light of the righteous* (Prov. XIII, 9). (T. B. Chagigah, 12a).

In contrast to the ordinary theological view, the idea is put forward in many sayings that the universe was formed not out of nothing but out of objects already existing, viz. the six elements mentioned in the beginning of Genesis —*tohu*, *bohu*, darkness, water, wind, and abyss (*tehom*), which preceded the creation.

In the following saying man is placed not only at the end but also in the beginning and at the centre of the creation : " R. Joshua b. R. Nehemiah and R. Judah b. R. Simon in R. Lazar's name said : He created him filling the whole world. How do we know . . . from east to west ? Because it is said : *Thou hast formed me behind and before* (Psalm CXXXIX, 5). And how do we know that he filled the empty spaces of the world ? From the words . . . *and laid Thy hand upon me* (*Ib.*). R. Lazar interpreted it : He was the latest (*achor*) in the work of the last day and the earliest (*kedem*) in the work of the last day.[6] That is R. Lazar's view, for he said, *Let the earth bring forth a soul of a living creature* (Genesis I, 24) refers to the soul of Adam. R. Simeon b. Lakish maintained : He was the latest in the work of the last day and the earliest in the work of the first day. That is consistent with the (other) view of R. Simeon b. Lakish, for he said : *And the Spirit of God hovered* (*Ib.* I, 2) refers to the soul of Adam, as you read, *And the spirit of God shall rest upon him* (Is. XI, 2)." (Ber. Rabba, VIII, 1.)

The importance of the Sabbath, which in the Bible itself appears first not as the subject of a commandment but as the crowning point of the creation, is brought out in the following similes. " Rabbi " (i.e. R. Judah the Prince) " asked R. Ishmael b. Jose : ' Have you heard from your father the actual meaning of *And on the seventh day God finished* ' ? He said to him : ' It is like a man striking a hammer on an anvil, raising it by day and bringing it down after nightfall.' . . . Genibah said : ' This may be compared to a king who made a bridal chamber which he plastered, painted, and adorned ; now what did the bridal chamber lack ? A bride to enter it. Similarly, what did the world still lack ? The Sabbath.' The Rabbis said : ' Imagine a king who made a ring. What did it lack ? A signet.

Similarly, what did the world lack ? The Sabbath.'" (Ber. Rabba, X, 9.)

Another practice of the Agada is to expand the element of mysticism which is to be found in some parts of the biblical narrative itself, as for instance when Melchizedek, the priestly king of Salem (i.e., Jerusalem), who mysteriously blessed Abraham with bread and wine, is identified with Shem the son of Noah,[7] who on his side is proclaimed as priestly descendant of the first man by the fact that he has received from Noah the priestly robes of Adam. Again, the mysterious ram which is offered in place of Isaac is reckoned among those things which were created at dusk on the sixth day before the Sabbath, and of its two horns—of which the shofar is meant to remind us—the left was the horn blown by God on Mount Sinai, while the right will one day be blown by Him on the day of the gathering of all the dispersed of Israel.[8]

The origin of Mosaism is brought into connection with the Creation by the statement that Moses during his stay in Midian drew from the ground a rod set with sapphire stones[9] on which was engraved the name of God. This was the rod with which the work of creation was completed. Adam took it with him out of Paradise, and eventually it reached Joseph, and came through the Egyptian princes to Jethro, who planted it in his garden and promised his daughter Zipporah to anyone who should draw it from the ground.[10]

Naturally a prominent place is taken in the Agada by the figure of Elijah, on account of his close connection with the Messiah. Leo Ginsberg sums up the legends relating to him as follows : "Elijah's preparatory work will be begun three days before the advent of Messiah. Then he will appear in Palestine and will utter a lament over the devastation of the Holy Land, and his wail will be heard throughout the world. The last words of his elegy will be, 'Now peace will come upon earth.' When the evildoers hear this message they will rejoice. On the second day he will appear again and proclaim : 'God will come upon earth.' And in the third his promise will be heard : ' Salvation will come upon earth.' Then Michael will blow the trumpet and once more Elijah will make his appearance, this time to introduce the Messiah."[11] And again : . . . " The Messiah will have Elijah blow the trumpet, and at the first sound the primal light, which shone before the week of the creation, will reappear ; at the second sound the dead will arise and with the swiftness of the wind assemble round the Messiah from all corners of the earth ; at the third sound the Shekinah will become visible to all ; the mountains will be razed at the fourth sound, and the Temple will stand in complete perfection as Ezekiel described it."[12]

It goes without saying that everywhere in the Agada and Midrash there is talk of angels, of a " future world ", of miracles and magical occurrences in daily life.[13] Statements of this nature, couched in a popular form, could have had their origin only in some more definite, conscious and systematic mystical teaching.

2.   Philo

Philo (Hebrew Jedidiah) was the most distinguished representative of the Jewish Hellenism which flourished in Alexandria during the last two centuries of the Second Temple. In his various exegetical works on the Pentateuch he carried to its highest point the allegorical method of interpreting the Pentateuch, which had been adopted by the Greek-speaking Jews of Alexandria, and which differed fundamentally from that in vogue among the Jewish scholars of Palestine. He sought above all things to show that the moral teaching of the Torah coincided with all that was best in Greek philosophy.[14] But he also wove into his system certain mystical doctrines, some of which are analogous to those contained in the Palestinian Agada. Whether Philo and the Agada exercised any direct influence on one another or drew from the same sources it is impossible to say.

As points which they have in common may be instanced the emphasis laid by them upon light as preceding the whole of the creation, and the idea that the visible universe before its appearance already existed in the mind of God like the plan of a building in the mind of an architect.[15]   The Agadic conception of the central importance of man in the scheme of creation may be paralleled by the statement of Philo that man is a kind of heaven in which the qualities correspond to the stars.   Again, in saying that the material from which the first man was made was taken from the best of the whole earth, he merely repeats a Midrash of the Pirke de R. Eliezer (ch. 12) which says that God took the dust for the first man from the four ends of the earth.   He also concurs with the Agada in explaining the word " place " used in the stories of Abraham, Jacob, and Moses (Genesis XXII, 4 ; Genesis XXVIII, 11 ; Exodus XXXIII, 21) to refer to the omnipresence of the Deity (*cf.* Ber. Rabba, 68, and Midrash Tehillim, 90).[16]   Philo also interprets the numbers mystically, but in the Pythagorean rather than the Jewish manner.   His treatment too of the life and immortality of the soul, while mystical, is strongly coloured by Platonic ideas.

The chief mystical element in the teaching of Philo is the idea of the Logos, as we are able to piece it together from various scattered passages in his writings.   The word *logos* is of course the translation of the biblical *dabar*, to which the Rabbis also gave a deep mystical significance, though as used by Philo it corresponds more to the *Memra* of the Targum (*v. supra*, p. 20).   Philo, however, in his elaboration of the logos idea, took a somewhat different line from the Palestinian teachers, and consequently his logos teaching had little influence on subsequent mystical thought in Judaism, though it profoundly affected that of Christianity.   He uses the word in more than one sense, and even on occasion speaks of a number of *logoi* (e.g., as a designation of the angels).   The Logos can be for him the instrument of creation, even the first-created or the Creator himself ;   the leader of the angels, who is also identical with the primordial man ; also the created world as a totality, and man himself when he attains to the highest stage of the priesthood. Keferstein, rather more philosophically, distinguishes the various meanings of *logos* as the idea out of which both the spiritual and sensible world develops ; as nature-power ; as world-spirit ; and as person.

These remarks may be illustrated by the following passages :

1. . . . " But if there be any as yet unfit to be called a son of God, let him press to take his place under God's firstborn, the Word who holds the eldership among the angels, their ruler as it were. And many names are his, for he is called " the Beginning " and " the Name of God " and His " Word " and " the Man after His image ", and " He that sees ", that is, Israel. . . . For if we have not yet become fit to be thought sons of God, yet we may be sons of His invisible image, the most holy Word. For the Word is the eldest-born image of God." . . . (The Confusion of Tongues, 146, 147).

2. . . . " Let us leave these merely particular buildings and contemplate that greatest of houses or cities, this universe. We shall see that its cause is God by whom it has come into being, its material the four elements from which it was compounded, its instrument the Word of God through which it was framed, and the cause of the building is the goodness of the architect (Demiurgos)." (De Cherubim, 127.)

3. . . . " Bezalel means then, ' in the shadow of God ' ; but God's shadow is His Word which He made use of like an instrument, and so made the world. But this shadow and what we may describe as the representation is the archetype for further creation. For just as God is the pattern of the image to which the title of shadow has just been given, even so the Image became the pattern of other beings." . . . (Allegorical Interpretations, III, 96.)

4. . . . " But let Melchizedek instead of water offer wine and give to souls strong drink that they may be seized by a divine intoxication more sober than sobriety itself. For he is a priest, even Logos, having as his portion Him

that is, and all his thoughts of God are high and vast and sublime ; for he is Priest of the Most High (Genesis XIV, 18)—not that there is any other not Most High, for God being one is ' in heaven above and on earth beneath, and there is none beside Him ' (Deuteronomy IV, 39) ; but to conceive of God not in low earth-bound ways but in lofty terms such as transcend all other greatness and all else that is free from matter, calls up in us a picture of the Most High." (*Ib.* III, 79, 82.)

5. . . . " Having said what was fitting on these matters, Moses continues : ' the bird he did not divide ' (Genesis XV, 10). He gives the name of bird to the two words (*logoi*), both of which are winged and of a soaring nature. One is the archetypical one above us, the other the copy of it which we possess. Moses calls the first the image of God, the second the cast of that image. For God, he says, made man not the image of God, but ' after the image ' (Genesis I, 27). And thus the mind in each of us, which in the true and full sense is the ' man ', is an expression at third hand from the Maker, while the middle one is a model for our reason, but itself the effigies or presentment of God." (Who is the Heir, 230, 231.)

6. . . . " For God, not condescending to come down to the external senses, sends His own Words or angels for the sake of giving assistance to those who have virtue. . . . Very properly, therefore, when he (Jacob) has arrived at the external senses, he is represented no longer as meeting God, but only the divine Word, just as his grandfather Abraham, the model of wisdom, did, for the Scripture tells us : ' And the Lord went His way as soon as He had left community with Abraham, and Abraham returned unto his place.' " (On Dreams, I, 12.)

Quite in the Jewish spirit is Philo's high estimation of Moses, whose law is described as a reflection and continuation of the law in accordance with which heaven and earth were created. Thus, commenting on the first chapter of Genesis he says : " And his (Moses') exordium is most admirable, embracing the creation of the world, under the idea that the law corresponds to the world and the world to the law, and that a man who is obedient to the law, being, by so doing, a citizen of the world, arranges his actions with reference to the intentions of nature, in harmony with which the whole universal world is regulated." (On the Creation of the World, ch. I.)

Weinstein in a penetrating study has pointed out a number of parallels between the Logos idea of Philo and certain teachings of the Agada.[17] Here we may rather point to certain important differences. For one thing, Philo is uniform in his terminology, using almost invariably the term *logos*, and at most adding the Platonic term *Demiurgos* to denote the creator, whereas the Agada has various designations for a highest created being standing between God and man and above the angels—Metatron, Michael, Melchizedek, or Shechinah. Again, Philo describes the nature of the Logos more rationally, while the Agada takes refuge in the enigmatical statements of the Bible, or, in the case of the Shechinah, in what appear to be popular conceptions. Historically, however, the most important difference is that Philo embraces the logos idea as a positive doctrine, whereas the Agada shows some uncertainty with regard to it. Thus for instance we have on the one hand the bold assertion of R. Akiba (Chag. 14a) that the second throne in the vision of Daniel (Dan. VII. 9) belongs to David, i.e., the Messiah, or the reference of the name YHWH in the account of Moses' ascent of God (Ex. XXIV, 1) to Metatron (San. XXX, 38b), while on the other side the inference hesitatingly drawn by Elisha ben Abuya from this statement, that the world is guided by two powers, is denounced as heresy. Possibly this ambiguous attitude, contemporaneous as it was with the beginnings of Christianity, reflects something of the attitude of the Judaism of the day to the budding new religion.

3. APOCALYPTIC LITERATURE

While mysticism appears in the Agada and Midrash only incidentally, and while it constitutes only one, though an important element in the system of Philo, it is of the very essence of the so-called apocalyptic literature, which begins with passages in certain books of the Bible (Isaiah, Ezekiel, Joel, Amos, Zephaniah, Zechariah, Malachi), is continued in a large number of writings which have not been included in the biblical canon, and reappears in the New Testament in the Apocalypse of St. John, though it assumes Christian forms in many other works also.[18]

The principal theme in these highly imaginative compositions is a picture of the future and the latter end of Israel and mankind, preceded always by a glimpse, vouchsafed to the mystic in a dream or vision, into the suprasensual world of God and the angels. This same theme formed a principal part, as we shall afterwards see, of that section of the oldest Jewish mystical teaching which is known as "Maaseh Merkabah". There, however, it appears in the form of doctrine; in the apocalyptic literature it takes the form of narratives of human or almost superhuman personalities to whom such a vision has been vouchsafed. These are figures from the biblical tradition, Adam, Abraham, Isaac, the twelve sons of Jacob ("Testament of the twelve Patriarchs"), Moses, Elijah, Baruch the disciple of the prophet Jeremiah, Zephaniah, Daniel, Ezra, and above all the striking figure of Enoch, of whom we read in the Bible that he did not die, but that God took him from earth, and who as "the Lad" (*Naar*) with the name of Metatron was elevated to the chief place among all the angelic beings.[19] The book which bears his name (and which exists in various versions and languages) is in some ways the *locus classicus* of the "Maaseh Merkabah".

In the apocalyptic writings the main theme of the heavenly vision is usually introduced with the story of an angel (in the "Apocalypse of Abraham" Jehoel, in the Book of Jubilees the Angel of the Presence, in one of the Enoch books Uriel)[20] being sent by God in order to reveal to a human being a glimpse into the heavenly world and therewith into the higher mysteries. This step may be regarded as the initiation of the human being concerned (who may be a contemporary, as Rabbi Ishmael in the Book of Enoch). Next is described the gradual ascent of the soul to heaven by various stages in which it is met by the angelic beings of the Book of Ezekiel, to the accompaniment of mysterious occurrences and apparitions from the upper world. These include the angelic hosts, the " Merkabah ", as a chariot drawn by, or rather a chorus consisting of various beings of different shapes and ranks, the angels of the elements and the stars and the guardian angels of the peoples, the watchers at the gates of the various heavens, the four archangels Michael, Uriel, Gabriel, and Raphael, and over all the Throne of God. Here and there too it is intimated that man sometimes can ascend to or at least behold higher regions than an angel.

With the ascent is sometimes joined a review of the biblical history (e.g. in the Book of Jubilees), and particularly a vista of the distant future. This often (e.g., in the Fourth Ezra and in the Apocalypse of Baruch) leads to a scene—sometimes drawn with dramatic power—in which the doubts and fears of the trembling human being are countered by the Deity or by the angelic guide with words of encouragement or correction or comfort. In awe-inspiring language the future destiny of Israel is unrolled (in Fourth Ezra and Baruch) along with the final decisive events of the far-distant future, as also the resurrection of the dead, effected by the heaven-sent Messiah. The details are filled in with a wealth of imagination which anticipates the visions of Dante in its pictures both of the joys of Paradise and of the punishments of the godless.[21]

The apocalyptic vision lays particular stress on the date which is fixed by the upper world for its fulfilment, and which man can neither hasten nor defer. It also introduces such subsidiary themes as popular legends (e.g., in the Apocalypse of Abraham), or explanations of physical, meteorological, and astronomical phenomena. One of the points which brings it into contact with Jewish mysticism is the occasional emphasising of the letters of the alphabet as creative elements, as also a tendency to anthropomorphism in describing the revelations of the Deity. It also shows a fondness for the gigantic in measurements of time and space, a feature which it has in common with Indian mysticism.

In such beings as Metatron and the Messiah (who here and there, as in the Apocalypse of Elijah, is designated in Christian fashion " son of God "), as also in the Shechinah (in the Books of Enoch) we meet again with appearances of the Deity in forms which conflict with a strict monotheism. This fact, together with the boldness of the symbolism, which to us to-day seems not a little startling, explains why the apocalyptic element in general remained more or less outside the sphere of Jewish religious development. While this religion aimed at a sanctification of the earthly life through a moral and religious law which was the same for all, the apocalyptic literature loses itself in contemplation of the heavenly spaces or in far-off vistas of the end of days, or of remote futurity. It belongs to a time when the outlook into the immediate future on earth was so dark that it had to be counterbalanced by bright visions of realms supernal or of the millennium—a point of view which the circumstances of our own time are rendering only too intelligible.

None the less in many respects the apocalyptic teaching has left its mark on Jewish mysticism, and even the Jewish liturgy. That the apocalyptic element in the Old Testament should have influenced deeply not only Jewish but also Christian religious development goes without saying. Christianity has laid particular stress on the prophecies of Isaiah regarding the " servant of YHWH ", the virgin birth of Immanuel (ch. VII), and the man of sorrows, "who is brought like a lamb to the slaughter " (ch. LIII) ; while for Judaism also the obscure chronological data, the world-kingdoms and the symbolical evil beasts of the Book of Daniel have formed the basis of Messianic speculations.[22] The angels of whom such vast numbers are named in the apocalyptic literature appear again in the so-called Hechalot literature, of which we shall speak in the next chapter, bearing the same descriptions. What is more, the angels' glorification of God described in the Books of Enoch—which is only an expansion of the wonderful visions in Isaiah VI, and Ezekiel III—forms the groundwork of the *Kedushah* hymns which are so important a part of the synagogue service. There is no ground at all for placing the origin of the *kedushah*, as Graetz does,[23] in the gaonic period, seeing that the main lines of the liturgy are already to be found in the Talmud, in Tractate Berachoth, while on the other hand the kedushah itself as a kind of angels' liturgy is already found in the Books of Enoch, as also in the Apocalypse of Abraham (*v.* p. 37).

NOTES TO CHAPTER II

[1] The word Agada (אגדא) is the Aramaic translation of the Hebrew Haggadah (הגדה) and means literally "telling" or "story". It is applied to all that part of the Talmud which does not come under the head of Halachah, or legal statement and discussion, and hence includes saga, legend, anecdote, and philosophical and mystical reflections. To the Agada in this extended sense belongs by far the greater part of the so-called Midrashic literature.

[2] Hence there is also a halachic midrash, and even a massoretic, concerned purely with textual questions.

[3] Most of this has been translated into German by August Wünsche under the title " Kleine Midrashim ".

[4] *V. supra*, p. 19.

[5] An intimation that such dicta belong to a secret tradition.

[6] The words נפש חיה in Gen. I, 24, being referred to the original man.

[7] The figure of Melchizedek, closely connected with that of Shem, plays a principal part in the Syrian-Christian "Treasure Cave" and the cognate " Book of Adam ".

[8] *V.* Ben Gorion, " Die Sagen der Juden," II, 295, 296.

[9] The mystical significance of the sapphire is shown by its mention in the account of the vision of the elders (Ex. XXIV, 10) and of Ezekiel (Ezek. I, 26). According to the Midrash the two Tables of the Law were also made of sapphire stone.

[10] Ben Gorion, *op. cit.*, III, 73–76. With this legend may be compared that of the North German mythology—springing of course from a quite different mental outlook—in which Sigurd (Siegfried) draws the broken sword of his father Sigmund from the earth.

[11] " Legends of the Jews," IV, 233, 234.

[12] *Ib.*, from Apocalypse of Daniel.

[13] On this point *cf.* especially Gideon Brecher, " Magie und magische Heilarten im Talmud ".

[14] *V.* Schürer, " History of the Jewish People in the Time of Jesus Christ " Vol. III.

[15] *V.* Index.

[16] The allegorical interpretation given by Philo to the manna (מן = " What ? "), as signifying the Reason of God, may be compared with the analogous interpretations given in the Zohar (I, 1b) to the words מי (= " Who ? ") and מה (= " What ? ").

[17] N. J. Weinstein, " Zur Genesis der Agada," *v.* Index.

[18] E.g., in the Testament of Isaac, the Apocalypse of Elijah, the Journey to Heaven of Isaiah, etc.

[19] The designation " Naar " arises from the application of the words חנוך לנער in Prov. XXII, 6, to Enoch.

[20] An analogous part is played by the angel Raziel in the cabbalistic work bearing that name, *v.* p. 70.

[21] *V.* Dods, " Forerunners of Dante ".

[22] *V.* A. H. Silver, " A History of Messianic Speculations in Israel " and *cf.* p. 136.

[23] *V.* H. Graetz " Die mystische Literatur in der geonischen Epoche ".

III

FIRST TRACES OF A JEWISH MYSTICAL DOCTRINE

APART from the mystical elements in the Agada, in the apocalyptic literature, and in allegorical bible exegesis with which we dealt in the previous chapter, there existed in the talmudical period[1] a Jewish mystical doctrine in the strict sense of the term. This fact is known to us first from the specific mention in the Talmud of certain mystical teachings ; secondly, from accounts, often legendary, of sects, schools, and individuals, to whom such doctrines were attributed ; thirdly, from literary documents—books, treatises, or isolated sayings—which contain such teaching.

The first Mishnah of the second chapter of the talmudical treatise Chagigah (On Festivals) lays down a prohibition to discuss sexual regulations with three persons, *Ma'aseh Bereshith*, i.e. the mysteries of the story of the Creation, with two, and *Ma'aseh Merkabah*, i.e., the mysteries of the celestial realms (as described in the vision of Ezekiel) even with one. In the discussion on this passage in the Gemara[2] this prohibition is modified in respect of certain classes of persons, and in regard to the Merkabah mysteries the exact passages in the Bible (Ezekiel I) to which it applies are specified, while the prohibition in general is based on the broad principle of the need to observe secrecy in certain matters. Thus in the same Mishnah we read : " Whoever turns his attention to four things, what is above, what is below, what is before, and what is behind, such a one were better not to have been born, being one who has not proper respect for the honour of his Creator." In another place in the same chapter the secret doctrine is designated " Sitre Torah ", —" mysteries of the Torah ". Elsewhere we read that four scholars penetrated into the " Pardes " (=Paradise),[3] and this term too seems to be used as a name for the secret doctrine. This doctrine, however, is here assigned to the

Agada, which, as we have seen, covered a very wide range of subjects.[4]

Generally speaking the Talmud, which always insists strongly on reverence for authority, shows, as already indicated, a twofold attitude to mysticism. On the one hand it recognises certain personalities as so to speak qualified mystics, making them the subject of legends and recording their sayings. Others again it stigmatises as heretics, in so far as through the study of mysticism they were led to become hostile or indifferent to the halachic law, or otherwise to adopt bold views which conflicted with strict monotheism.[5] This was especially the case with Elisha b. Abuya, who on this account received the name of " Acher " (Another).

The reason for this rejection of the mystic doctrine, or, rather, for the insistence on keeping it strictly secret, was a recognition of the danger which lay in any wrong or one-sided idea of it. Thus we find in the Gemara of the Jerusalem Talmud on this same Mishnah : " Rabbi (i.e., Rabbi Judah the Prince) had a worthy disciple who once recited before him a passage from the Merkabah mystery. Rabbi did not agree with it, and he was smitten with boils. This mystical doctrine can be compared to two paths, one of which leads into fire (or " light "), the other into ice (or " snow "). Whoever strays into the former perishes in fire, and whoever strays into the latter perishes in ice. What should the student do ? He should walk in the middle." And of the four scholars mentioned above it is recorded : " Our Rabbis taught : Four men entered the Garden, namely, Ben Azzai and Ben Zoma, Acher and R. Akiba. R. Akiba said to them : When ye arrive at the stones of pure marble, say not : Water, water.[6] For it is said : *He that speaketh falsehood shall not be established before mine eyes* (Psalm CI, 7). Ben Azzai cast a look and died. Of him Scripture says : *Precious in the eyes of the Lord is the death of His saints* (Psalm CXVI, 15). Ben Zoma looked and became demented. Of him Scripture says : *Hast thou found honey ? Eat as much as is sufficient for thee, lest thou be filled therewith and vomit it* (Prov. XXV, 16). Acher mutilated the shoots. R. Akiba went up unhurt and went down unhurt." (Chagigah, 14*b*).

To the still earlier devotees of the Jewish mystic lore belonged, according to Josephus and Philo, the Essenes,[7] who possessed books of mysteries and knew secrets which they did not dare to disclose. These related to the four-lettered name of God (the tetragrammaton) and the other names of the Deity, as also to those of the angels. For the Essenes and also, as it would appear, for the Therapeutæ,[8] mysticism formed the kernel of the teaching which regulated their half communistic, half monastic way of life, and of which scrupulous cleanliness in clothing and food, industry, systematic daily routine, homage to light, and particular veneration of the Sabbath, were the chief features.

Among the sects of the talmudic and even of the pre-talmudic period who seem to have had mystical leanings, but concerning whom nothing beyond a few casual references has come down to us, Abelson reckons the " Silent Ones " (*Chashaim*), from whom possibly the name " Essenes " was derived, and who were also called " Fearers of Sin " (*Yir'e Het*) ; the " Worthy Ones " (*Vatikin*), also called the " Humble " (*Anavim*), who were prayer mystics ; and the " Chaste " (*Zenu'im*), who occupied themselves with letter-mysticism.

The leaders of the Essenes have remained completely unknown to us, but in the Talmud we learn by name of certain possessors of a mystic tradition who came from the ranks of the Pharisees. These men exhibit for the most part a double character, since many of them are at the same time prominent representatives of the strict ritual-halachist point of view. It would seem that within the larger schools of scholars there were formed special circles for the cultivation of the secret doctrine,[9] consisting of scholars who in other respects also were in close contact with each other. Probably the great Rabbi Johanan ben Zakkai, the spiritual leader of the people at the time of the destruction of the Temple, became the head of such a circle, which was later

joined by his disciples R. Joshua b. Chananyah, R. Jose, who
is mentioned specifically as being versed in the knowledge of
the Merkabah, R. Eliezer the Great, and above all his disciple,
R. Akiba. To the mystics belonged further R. Eleazar b.
Arak, R. Ishmael, and the Rabbis mentioned in the Pardes
legend, and also the Amora Abba Areka (Rab). If we can
attach any historical value to the statements of the Zohar,
a similar circle was again formed by R. Simeon b. Yochai,
with his son R. Eleazar, R. Abba, R. Judah, R. Jose, R.
Jesse, R. Isaac, R. Chiyah, and R. Pinchas b. Jair as members.[10] We find also occasional mention of other mystics
or wonder-workers, such as R. Chaninah and R. Nechunyah
b. Hakaneh, besides the scholars mentioned in the Book
of Bahir.[11]

The spirit in which the mystic doctrine was approached
by those who cultivated it is illustrated by legends, mostly
relating to the Merkabah, and of which the following are
specimens.

" The Rabbis taught : There was once a child who was
reading at his teacher's house the Book of Ezekiel, and
he apprehended what Chashmal was, whereupon a fire
went forth from the Chashmal and consumed him. So they
sought to suppress the Book of Ezekiel, but Chananyah b.
Hizkiah said to them : If he was a Sage all are Sages . . ."
(Here follow two interpretations of the rare word *Chashmal*,
which is used in Ezek. I, 4, 27, to denote a sort of heavenly
fire or splendour.)

" Our Rabbis taught : Once R. Johanan b. Zakkai was
riding on an ass when going on a journey, and R. Eleazar b.
Arak was driving the ass from behind. R. Eleazar said to
him : ' Master, teach me a chapter from the " Work of the
Chariot " ' . He answered : ' Have I not taught you thus :
Nor the Work of the Chariot in the presence of one unless
he is a Sage and understands of his own knowledge ? '
(R. Eleazar) then said to him : ' Master, permit me to say
before thee something which thou hast thyself taught me.'
He answered : ' Say on.' Forthwith R. Johanan b. Zakkai
dismounted from his ass and wrapped himself up and sat

upon a stone beneath an olive tree. Said (R. Eleazar) to him : 'Master, wherefore didst thou dismount from the ass?' He answered : 'Is it proper that whilst thou are expounding the "Work of the Chariot" and the Divine Presence is with us and the Ministering Angels accompany us I should ride on the ass?' Forthwith R. Eleazar b. Arak began his exposition of the "Work of the Chariot", and fire came down from the heaven and encompassed all the trees in the field. Thereupon they all began to utter (divine) song. What was the song they uttered? *Praise the Lord from the earth, ye sea-waters and all deeps . . . fruitful trees and all cedars, hallelujah* (Psalm CXLVIII, 7, ff). An angel then answered from the fire and said : 'This is the very Work of the Chariot. Happy art thou, O Abraham our father, that R. Eleazar b. Arak has come from thy loins. . . .'

Now when these things were told R. Joshua, he and R. Jose the Priest were going on a journey. They said : ' Let us also expound the Work of the Chariot.' So R. Joshua began an exposition. Now that day was the summer solstice ; (nevertheless) the heaven became overcast with clouds and a rainbow appeared in the cloud, and the Ministering Angels assembled and came to listen, like people who assemble and come to watch the entertainments of a bridegroom and bride." (Chagigah, 14*b*.)

From the nature of the subject itself and from the sayings that have been transmitted to us it is evident that this doctrine occupied itself largely with those difficulties in the biblical account which the rational intelligence finds most perplexing. In the story of the Creation these concern principally the light—that is, the contrast between the light which on the first day sprang from the word of the Creator and that of the heavenly bodies which were not created till the fourth day ; the seven " days ", which obviously are days not of man but of God ; the meaning of the upper and lower waters and of the *rakia* between them ; the exact place of man in the scheme of creation, and, further, the differences between the two accounts of the creation of man in the first and second chapters. Much has come down to us on these subjects only in the form of Agadic Midrash. The mystic interpretation, however, emphasises much more strongly the macrocosmic nature of the original man—who finds a parallel in the Persian-Manichean "Gavra Kadmaya"—distinguishing him from the "first man" (Adam ha-rishon), and assigning to him some messianic features.[12] The mystic doctrine of the Creation further attaches a literal meaning to the " word " as the instrument of creation in so far as it seeks for traces of this " word " in the properties of the written letters and their sounds. If we add to these features the importance assigned to the division of the material universe into four fundamental elements—the concepts of which were taken over from Greek philosophy—the idea of gradations in the scale of existence,[13] and the attribution to numbers of formative power, we have summed up the teaching of the Sefer Yezirah (lit. " Book of Formation "), a document of great significance for the development of mysticism, and the origins of which go back to a high antiquity.

The Sefer Yezirah, though containing only six short chapters, is in many respects one of the most notable works in Jewish literature. It might be called the earliest scientific treatise in the Hebrew language ; it is the earliest systematic treatment of the Jewish mystical doctrine, containing also the germs of a system of Hebrew phonetics and of a natural philosophy and physiology based on that doctrine. It has come down to us in two versions[14] written in a terse and vigorous Hebrew[15] which seems to date from the period immediately following that of the Bible or from that of the Mishnah, though a slightly foreign flavour is lent to it by the admixture of terms borrowed from Greek. After the manner of old oriental meditative writings its style is strictly rhythmical, though quite unpoetical, and it is almost devoid of any ethical-religious element. Its connection with the Merkaba-mysticism is shown by its frequent reference to the Merkabah chapter in the Bible (Ezekiel I), which seems also to a certain extent to have affected its terminology.

We shall have occasion to deal more in detail with the
date, origin, and authorship, of the Sefer Yezirah in connection with the growth of the Cabbalah. It will be sufficient
here to refer to the legend mentioned in the Talmud that
with its help two scholars, R. Oshaiah and R. Chaninah,
created a three-year-old calf (San. 65b and 67b), and that
R. Joshua b. Chananyah in the same way produced deer
and fawns from cucumbers and pumpkins (T. J., San. VII,
154), which can be taken to imply that the study of this
book, or at any rate its magical use, confers on the adept
creative powers. Certainly the book must have already been
well known in the ninth century, since two commentaries
on it have come down to us from this period, one by
the celebrated Gaon Saadia and the other by Sabbatai
Donolo.

The subject of the book is the creation, or, more strictly
speaking, the formation of the world " in thirty-two ways
of wisdom ", represented by the twenty-two letters of the
Hebrew alphabet and the ten numbers of the first decade,
which are called " sefiroth ". This act of creation is also
pictured as a kind of emanation from a supreme entity, the
Holy Spirit, into the three superior elements.[16] As might
be expected from a doctrine which attaches so much importance to sounds, the central element is air, from which fire
springs upwards as basis of the heavenly world and water
downwards as basis of the material world.

The twenty-two letters are grouped into three " Mothers "
(Aleph, Mem, Shin), seven double signs (i.e., with dual
pronunciation), and twelve simple signs. The three
" mothers " correspond to the three elements already
named, air, fire, and water, the seven double signs to the
planets, and the twelve simple ones to the signs of the
Zodiac. This division has a threefold application in the
cosmology of the Sefer Yezirah—to time (in the form of
" year "), to space (in the form of the macrocosm) and to
human organism (in the form of the microcosm). In Hebrew
these are denominated נפש עולם שנה. Thus as applied to
man this threefold arrangement denotes a division—which

is adopted also by modern anthroposophy[17]—into an upper part (the head), a middle (the breast), and a lower (the abdomen). Conformably, however, to the spirit of monotheism a supreme element is supposed to rule over all the divisions. Among the stars this is a figure, which has not yet been satisfactorily explained, called Teli (perhaps the constellation of the Dragon or the Polar star, or some archetypal form), and in the human organism the heart.

In many places in the book it is intimated that in the various combinations of letters, which are called "the building of houses"—that is to say, in fact, in the formation of words—there exists a principle parallel to the building up of things in the world out of their elements. The central point in this process is the formation of the name of God out of the permutations of its three letter-sounds. This is a typical example of the practical letter-mysticism which in general is called "*Zeruf*" (combination), and of which there are three main kinds, *Gematria, Notarikon,* and *Temurah.* *Gematria,* which was very widely used, rests on the numerical values of the letters, and its method is to bring into relation with one another words with the same numerical values. Thus the angel "in whom resides the name of God" (Ex. XXIII, 21) must be Metatron because the words Metatron (מטטרון) and Shaddai (שדי) have the same numerical value, viz. 314. Similarly both "Menachem" (מנחם) and "Zemach" (צמח), each with the numerical value of 138, denote the Messiah.[18] The method of the *Notarikon* is similar to that of the acrostic, and consists in making up new words from the first or last letters of others. Thus the mystics were known as *Yod'ei Chen* (knowers of God's grace),[19] because the first and last letters of the word *Chen* (grace) can be taken as the "notarikon" for *Chokhmah Nistarah* (hidden wisdom). Similarly the word *Pardes* is supposed to hint at the fourfold way of interpreting the Scripture, viz. literally (*Peshat*), allusively (*Remez*), allegorically (*Derush*), and mystically (*Sod*). *Temurah* finally denotes the alteration of a word by transposing its letters. Thus in the Sefer Yezirah the words *Oneg* (=עֹנֶג delight) and *Nega'* (=נֶגַע, pain), which consist of the same letters, are opposed to one another.[20]

The second main field of the earliest Jewish mystical doctrine, viz. the Merkabah teaching, is intimately connected with the first chapter of the Book of Ezekiel, i.e., with the " divine visions " (v. 1), in which the " glory of God " reveals itself to the prophet, and which are described with an imagery, and to some extent in language, differing from those of other prophetic visions recorded in the Bible. The prophet feels himself carried away by a tempest coming from the north (v. 4) into a heavenly sphere, in the midst of cloud, fire, and lightning ; and in fact a lightning and illumination of an unearthly kind plays around the whole world of these visions[21] (vv. 4, 27). As in the ascent to heaven of Moses (Ex. XXIV), ice, sapphire, and rainbow build the horizon of this heaven, in which the beholder observes with trembling and ecstasy the mighty movement of an angelic chorus.

In addition to the names Cherubim and Seraphim applied elsewhere in the Bible to angels, we meet here with the designation *Chayoth*,[22] which is usually taken to mean holy beings in animal form. Inseparably joined to them are the Ophanim, whose name denotes some kind of wheel or revolving form ; this perhaps gave rise to the concept of the Merkabah (lit. carriage), a word which is not actually used in the Ezekiel vision itself.[23] The four " animals ", each one of which has four faces and is provided with wings (v. 6), present the fourfold appearance of a lion, an ox, an eagle, and a human being, though in some way the human trait is present in all the others (v. 5).

It is important to note that the angels are conceivable as being only in motion and not at rest, and the descriptive touches given by the prophet conform to this idea. Thus attention is called to the rectilinear movement and to the feet (vv. 17, 7), to the union of faces and wings (11), and to the turning of the faces under the guidance of the spirit (v. 12). Similarly the "wheels" (Ophanim) are represented as if there were "one wheel inside another" (v. 16), and as being joined to the Chayoth which move them by means of the spirit. The general picture is completed by a few details, as that the backs are full of eyes (v. 18), just as in the Johnian apocalypse. There is also the noise of the movement of the wings, "like the voice of mighty waters, like the voice of Shaddai" (v. 24), and another voice high over the heavenly dome (v. 25). The central point in the whole vision is the appearance of the Throne of God, and on it "a form like the appearance of a man" (v. 26). Thus at the highest point of the divine vision appears the form of man.

Four *Chayoth*, as also the human form on the divine throne, appear again in a dream[24] of Daniel (Dan. VII), in connection with a great apocalyptic vision of the end of days (the four evil beasts representing the four empires). This description, through its repetition in the Johnian apocalypse, which also brings in the four horses of the vision of Zechariah (Zech. VI, 2, 3), has had a great influence on the religious concepts and experiences of Christendom—more than on those of Judaism, though it has also affected the development of the Jewish Merkabah mysticism.[25]

The most important literary product of the Merkabah mysticism is the so-called Hechaloth literature. To this belong the larger and smaller Hechaloth (Hechaloth Rabbati and Zutrati), the tractate Midrash Konen, and the Shiur Komah.[26] Its most important constituent, however, is the Hebrew Book of Enoch, which, while itself the crowning point of the visionary apocalyptic literature, seems also to form the starting point of the genuinely Jewish Hechaloth mysticism. The word "Hechaloth" designates the "heavenly palaces" or special regions, especially that of the seventh heaven, "Araboth", where the experiences of Enoch are supposed to have taken place. In the tractate Chagigah (12*a*) this highest heaven is spoken of as follows : "Araboth is that in which there are right and judgment and righteousness, the treasures of life and the treasures of peace and the treasures of blessing, the souls of the righteous and the spirits and souls which are yet to be born, and dew wherewith the Holy One, blessed be He, will hereafter revive the dead. . . . There too are the Ophanim and the Seraphim and the Holy Living Creatures (Chayoth) and the Ministering Angels (Malache Ha-shareth) and the Throne of God, and the King, the Living God, high and exalted, dwells over them in Araboth, for it is said : *Extol Him that rideth upon Araboth whose name is the Lord* (Psalm LXVIII, 5). . . ."

In this Hechaloth literature, as in the kindred passages in the Talmud and Midrash, we meet with angelic beings in boundless profusion. The highest groups of angels are designated also " Household of the Upper World " (*Pamelia shel Ma'alah*) or Ministering Angels (*Mal'achei ha-Shareth*). In the works which relate journeys of the soul there appear at the gates of the various heavens special gatekeepers (porters), who also hand over the " seals " to those who are to be initiated. The Book of Daniel already mentions such beings as " Watchers and holy ones " (Dan. IV, 10, 14, 20).[27] In the Ethiopian Book of Enoch seven holy angels who keep watch are enumerated : Uriel, Raphael, Raguel, Michael, Zerachiel, Gabriel, and Remiel. Thus they include also the four principal angels (later called by the Christians " Archangels "), who in the fortieth chapter are represented as faces on the four sides of the Deity—Michael, Raphael, Gabriel, and Phanuel (otherwise Uriel). In the Hechaloth mention is also made of a " Prince of the Torah " (*Sar ha-Torah*) and " Prince of the Sanctuary " (*Sar Hakodesh*). In specially close contact with the presence of God is the " Prince of the Presence " (*Sar Ha-panim*—so called in the Book of Jubilees), perhaps identical with Michael.[28]

The evil angels or demonic beings also play in the whole of this literature, as in the Talmud, a not unimportant role as " Angels of Destruction " (*Malache Chabalah*) or as ubiquitously roving spirits (*Shedim*). To the most prominent evil powers belong Asmodai, the opponent of Solomon, Lilith (Adam's first wife), Dumah, the angel of the stillness of death, Beliar (perhaps from *bli-ya'al* = contemptible), and in the Johnian *Apocalypse* Sorath, bearer, under the system of Gematria, of the mysterious number 666, which was also applied to the Emperor Nero.

The formation of the names of the angels seems to follow certain definite rules. Along with Gabriel and Michael who are mentioned in the Bible and Raphael who is mentioned in the Book of Tobit we find principally names which similarly end with the termination *el* denoting divine power, and in addition signify the specific quality, mission or function of the angel concerned. Thus besides Jehoel (in the Apocalypse of Abraham) which is directly derived from the name of God, we have Uriel or Nuriel (fire), Zadkiel (righteousness), Zahariel (brightness), Akatriel (crown), and so forth. In the Hebrew Book of Enoch there are a vast number of such names which perhaps are *hapax legomena* formed with reference to definite experiences and their effects on the person concerned. In the later literature they may have been formed only with a view to producing certain magical effects.

The most striking figure in this angelic world is Metatron, into whom Enoch was changed after his transference to the heavenly spheres. He is the leader of all angels, standing so high over them that in the Hebrew Book of Enoch he is actually designated "lesser YHWH" (יהוה הקטן). As heavenly scribe, who registers the deeds and shortcomings of men, he reminds us of the Egyptian Thoth. He is also the heavenly advocate (*sanegor*, i.e. Gr. *synegoros*) for Israel, and the High Priest who brings offerings on the heavenly altar. From a number of parallel passages Weinstein has shown that it is possible to identify him with Michael, who also is represented as a heavenly High Priest, the true advocate of Israel, and as identical with the angel "in whom God's name resides" (Ex. XXIII, 21). Metatron may also be so far compared with the Logos of Philo that both can be conceived as a genuine reflection of the Deity, what would be called in the Christian-apocalyptic sense a "Son of God". Many other points of similarity adduced by Weinstein seem, however, to be rather arbitrary.[29]

The origin of the name Metatron is obscure. Many theories have been put forward, which are grouped by Odeberg as follows : (1) From the stem *natar*, to watch (Jellinek) ; (2) from the Latin "metator", measurer (Eleazar of Worms) ; (3) from the Persian God Mithra (Joel, Kohut) ; (4) from *mater, matrona*, which became in Aramaic *matronita*, one of the cabbalistic designations of the Shechinah (Levi b. Gerson) ; (5) from *meta thronon*," behind the Throne " (Ad. Frank, Oesterley and Box). In Hechalot Rabbati Metatron is identified with the "Angel Anaphiel ".[30]

The existence of a systematic Merkabah mysticism is proved by the mention of the so-called "Yorde Merkabah" (lit. "those who go down to the Merkabah "), both in the Hechaloth and also in a statement of Hai Gaon in the tenth century.[31] In both cases mention is made at the same time of a "vision of the Merkabah " (*zefiath ha-Merkabah*), and of certain methods for attaining to it, which again presuppose a rigorous course of moral and ascetic preparation. Sholem draws attention to the peculiar use in this connection of the term "descent ", which seems in a way to be opposed to the previously prevalent idea of an "ascent " of the soul. Perhaps this contrast corresponds to the contrast between an attitude of ecstatic self-effacement and one of conscious inquiry in the approach to the world of mystery. From the description in the Zohar cited above we may conclude that already in the talmudical period there were formal initiations.[32] Sholem mentions a special initiation rite which is described in the "Sefer ha-Malbush " as an "investing with the divine Name ", and in which the candidate has to put on a robe with the name of God woven into it.[33]

A passage from a Hechaloth tractate quoted by Sholem[34]

makes it clear that to each stage of initiation corresponded a stage in religious and moral progress. " R. Akiba said to R. Ishmael : When I ascended to the first palace I was devoted (*chassid*), in the second palace I was pure (*tahor*), in the third sincere (*yashar*), in the fourth I was wholly with God (*tamim*), in the fifth I displayed holiness before God, in the sixth I spoke the *kedushah* . . . before Him by whose word the world was created, in order that the guardian angels might not hurt me ; in the seventh palace I held myself erect with all my might, trembling in all limbs, and spoke the following prayer : ' Praise be to Thee who art exalted, praise be to the Sublime in the chambers of grandeur.' "

These visions of a multifarious angelic hierarchy find their completion—perhaps by way of contrast—in an apprehension of the mystical significance of the hidden name of God (*Shem Ha-meforash* שם המפרש), as handed down from the Temple service. The talmudic tradition distinguishes between the usual divine name of four letters, which is replaced in the prayers by the name *Adonai* and in conversation by " *ha-Shem* " (the Name) simply, later also by " *Adoshem* ", and a name of 42 or 72 letters,[35] the nature of which is still a problem. Possibly the number 72 was obtained by a triangular diminution of the name YHWH such as was practised by the Pythagoreans, and was called in Greek " klima ".[36] Besides these of course there were the numerous other biblical and post-biblical names of God, including some which, like many of the angels' names, were only formed for a special occasion.

On the other side the cult of the " Names " forms the core of a widespread mysticism of sounds and letters which ranges in its choice of subject from the cosmological speculations of the Sefer Yezirah to the fanciful personification of the letters of the alphabet contained in R. Akiba's " Midrash of the Letters " (אותיות דר עקיבא), printed by Jellinek[37] in two versions, and in a passage of the Zohar (Introduction, I, 2*b*) based on the second of these. The letters are here introduced, one after the other, beginning with the last, putting forth before God their claim to be used for commencing the creation of the world. The victory ultimately goes to the Beth (the first letter in the Torah), though in other respects the Aleph, the head of all the letters, is assigned pre-eminence. The letters H and Y from the Tetragrammaton are further distinguished by the fact that with the former the material world was created and with the latter the imperceptible point, the future world (v. Otiyoth di R. Akiba, also Bereshith Rabba, XII, 10, T. B. Menachoth, 29b, and the Zohar passim).

Among the most notable anonymous writings of this class is the " Shiur Komah " (lit. " Measure of Stature "), in which the members of the Godhead, or rather, as Sholem rightly points out, of its outward appearance, the Shechinah, are drawn in colossal dimensions, that is to say, in a number-symbolism which is no longer intelligible to us. There is also the " Sword of Moses " which was discovered and edited by Moses Gaster, and which consists largely of magic formulæ, the sword itself being formed of mystical divine names (ch. 2). We have here a good example of the way in which that which was originally mystical and visionary became capricious and magical, the angelic world being made the object of prayers which are no longer humble supplications to the Deity, but themselves aim at setting in motion magical powers in the upper world. This kind of mysticism is concerned not with the content of visions, still less with their rational understanding, but solely with the performance of magic ; and as Sholem points out, the less sense any passage has in itself, the more important it becomes for this purpose.[38]

We have already noted the redundance in texts of this kind of angelic names and formulæ of benediction. A similar redundance, but carried to much further lengths, meets us in the contemporary mystic, hymnal and liturgical literature. We find it already as a striking feature of the Hebrew Book of Enoch, but we also find it in the noble Nishmath prayer (which has been included in the morning service for Sabbath and holydays), and in the hymns inserted in the prayers, like those of Eleazar-ha-Kalir, and even in the introduction to the Sefer Yezirah.

NOTES TO CHAPTER III

[1] This covers a period of several centuries, from the first century before to the seventh century after the Christian era. It is divided into the periods of the Tannaim, who compiled the Mishnah (up to nearly the end of the 2nd century C.E.), the Amoraim, who compiled the Gemara (up to the end of the fifth century), and the Saboraim, the last editors of the Talmud.

[2] The Talmud consists of two parts, the Mishnah, which is a code of laws, and the Gemara, which contains discussions on the Mishnah and other matter relating to it. In our Talmud texts the Mishnah is divided into short passages each followed by its appropriate piece of Gemara.

[3] *V.* p. 43.

[4] Thus in Tractate Chagigah we read that after R. Akiba's interpretation of Dan. VII, 13, quoted above, R. Eliezer turned to him with the words : " Akiba, what have you to do with Agada ? Keep your observations for *negaim* and *ohaloth* " (lit. " plagues and tents," i.e., purely ritual matters).

[5] *V.* p. 36.

[6] Abelson interprets these words as a warning against adopting the Greek doctrine of Nature.

[7] *V.* Josephus, B. J., II, 8, §. 12 and 13 ; Ant. XIII, 5, § 9 ; *ib.* 10, §§4 and 5 ; Philo, " Quod Probus sit Liber," etc.

[8] The Therapeutæ were distinguished externally from the Essenes by the fact that they lived not in Palestine but in Egypt, and that they also included non-Jews. An internal difference according to Philo consisted in their more contemplative and less practical way of life. Of the Essenes he says : " who assiduously practise the life of action " ; of the Therapeutæ, " who embrace the life of contemplation ". Philo describes the Therapeutæ in detail in his work " De Vita Contemplativa ", which was discovered in 1895 by Conybeare. For further information on the Essenes *v.* Ginsberg, " The Essenes ", and on both sects the writings of Lucius (*v.* Index).

[9] On this subject *v.* Ad. Franck, " La Cabbale " ; Joel, " Die Religionsphilosophie des Sohar " ; and Sholem, " Major Trends in Jewish Mysticism," II ; also art. " Kabbalah " in the Encyclopædia Judaica.

[10] *V.* Zohar, III. 127*b*–128*a*.

[11] In later times it became usual to ascribe Cabbalistic writings to talmudic-mystical authorities, e.g. the " Otioth di R. Akiba " to Rabbi Akiba, the Book of Bahir to R. Nechunyah b. Hakaneh, and the Zohar to R. Simeon b. Yochai.

[12] *V.* the dictum of R. Simeon b. Lakish quoted on p. 30. Many versions, however, instead of " the soul of Adam " read " the spirit of the Messiah-king ".

[13] For the Cabbalistic four stages of creation *v.* p. 79.

[14] *V.* on this point Lazarus Goldschmidt, " Das Buch der Schöpfung ", Introduction.

[15] The Sefer Yezirah is fond of using words in their primary significance with special reference to sound-mysticism, e.g. *hakak* (" to stamp ") to represent one of the original creative activities. So too the root *sefer* is used to designate the original process of number-formation, and *nefesh*, as often in the Bible, not strictly of the soul but of the animated organism, etc.

[16] The highest stage of emanation is a kind of self-reproduction or self-mirroring. Hence in this stage " ruach " (which signifies both " spirit " and " air ") again springs from ruach (*v.* Sefer Yezirah, I, 9, 10).

[17] In the anthroposophic system the " lower man " denotes both the metabolic and the articulatory system, in so far as motion is dependent on metabolism. In the " upper man " are concentrated the functions of thought, in the middle one those of feeling, and in the lower one those of will.

[18] According to Thimus, " Die harmonikale Symbolik des Altertums ", the word Teli denotes the form of the cross. Thimus believes that the formulæ of the Sefer Yezirah represent an old esoteric tone-system.

[19] Other examples :—סולם (" ladder," with special reference to Jacob's ladder) has the same numerical value as סיני (Sinai). והנה שלשה (" and behold three ", of the three men who appeared to Abraham Gen. XVIII, 2) אלו מיכאל גבריאל ורפאל (these are Michael, Gabriel, Raphael). For other kinds of Gematria *v.* Ginsberg, " The Kabbalah ".

[20] The saying of God mentioned in the first chapter of Genesis is described by the Zohar as the combined working of אש (fire), מים (water) and רוח (air), the first three letters of which compose the word אמר, (he said). The final letters of the first three words of the Bible (בראשית ברא אלהים) compose the word אמת (" truth "), a fact which the Rabbis perhaps had in mind in describing truth as " the seal of God ". (Talm. Sabbat 55a). For other examples and methods *v.* Ginsberg.

[21] The word *Chashmal* (חשמל) used in this account, and denoting a kind of heavenly fire, constitutes a special mystery within the general mystery of the Merkabah. For a characteristic legend connected with it, *v.* quotation from Chagigah 13*a* on p. 45.

[22] Later the *Chayoth* were explained by the Zohar as beings from which life springs. On the other hand the reference to the animal faces in the vision is obvious. In many religions, especially the Egyptian, divine beings appear in animal form. According to the anthroposophic explanation, the four faces of the apocalyptic beasts are the original ethereal forms of the human nature.

[23] Though it might be taken from Zechariah, vi, 1–8. The term " Merkabah " was applied later to the ascent to heaven or the actual vision of the divine might. We even find seven Merkaboth mentioned, corresponding to the seven heavens.

[24] And so on a somewhat lower stage of inspiration. For the two thrones in Daniel, *v.* also p. 36.

[25] Some of the most characteristic terms of Jewish mysticism have been taken from the account of Daniel, which is in Aramaic, e.g., the " Ancient of Days " (עתיק יומין), the purifying stream of fire which

surrounds His throne (נהר די נור), and the " Holy Ones of the Highest " (קדישין עליונין), as a designation of angels. (עיירין קדישין) *v.* p. 69 (Note 14).

[26] First published in the " Bet-Hamidrash " collection of Ad. Jellinek.

[27] *V.* p. Note 25.

[28] In the apocalyptic as in the hechaloth literature we again meet with an incredible number of angelic beings. The number of the names of angels in the mystic-cabbalistic literature is so great that Moise Schwab was able to compile a lexicon of angels and demons merely from the material in the manuscripts in the Paris Bibliothèque Nationale.

[29] Referring to the words in Exodus, XXIV, 1, " And he said to Moses, Go up to YHWH ", the Talmud in Sanhedrin 38*b* says that the speaker here is Metatron, whereas the Targum Jonathan assigns these words to Michael. In Chagigah 12*b* it is stated in the name of Simeon b. Lakish that in the heaven called " Zebul " there is an upper Jerusalem, an upper Temple, and an upper altar at which " Michael the great prince " stands and brings offerings (*cf.* also Men, 110*a*, and Zebachim, 62*a*), which in the En Yakob collection are described more precisely as " the souls of the righteous ". On the other hand we find in Midrash Rabba to Num. XII : " At the moment when the Holy One, blessed be He, commanded Israel to erect the sanctuary, He intimated to the ministering angels that they should on their side at the same time also erect a sanctuary. This is the sanctuary of the " Lad " who is called Metatron, and in it he brings the souls of the pious as offerings, as an atonement for Israel in the days of their exile " (*V.* Weinstein, pp. 63–65). Analogous statements are to be found in the apocalyptic literature.

[30] *V.* Odeberg, pp. 125 *sqq.*

[31] The passage from the " Ozar Ha-Geonim " to Tractate Chagigah runs as follows : " Many scholars were of the belief that one who is distinguished by many qualities described in the books and who is desirous of beholding the Merkabah and the palaces of the angels on high must follow certain ways. He has to fast a number of days and lay his head between his knees and whisper down to the earth many hymns and songs known from tradition. Then he perceives the interior and the chambers, as seeing the seven palaces with his own eyes, and it is as though he entered one palace after the other and saw what is therein." The author of this passage remarks also that there are two treatises (Mishnayoth) dealing with these secrets—the Hechaloth Rabbati and Zutrati.

[32] *V.* Sholem, p. 69. In the Midrash ha-Neelam (Zohar, I, pp. 98, 99) there is direct mention of an initiation of R. Akiba into the mysteries of the Song of Songs and the Merkabah by the dying R. Eliezer. And in the Hechaloth Rabbati R. Akiba is expressly designated an initiate of the Merkabah.

[33] *V.* Sholem, p. 69.

[34] *V.* Sholem, p. 77.

[35] For more on this subject see L. Blau, " Altjüdisches Zauberwesen ". Also Daiches, " Babylonian Magic in the Talmud and in the later Jewish Literature ".

[36] In the following form:

יהוה	..	..	..	..	26
יהו	..	..	..	..	21
יה	..	..	..	..	15
י	..	..	..	..	10
					72

Ginsberg quotes other similar anagrams. See also H. L. Held, " Von Golem und Shem ". Among the best known anagrams are the Greek Abracadabra and the Hebrew Shabriri on amulets.

[37] In his " Beth Ha-Midrash " collection.

[38] That magic was practised with the names of God can also be seen from the Greek-Jewish magical texts originating in Egypt, which have been edited by Blau. These differ from similar Babylonian and Greek texts in the fact that here the Hebrew name of God (in the form IAO), along with angels' names, takes the place of the names of heathen deities.

IV

THE ORIGIN OF THE CABBALAH

THE name Cabbalah appears for the first time, as far as is
known, in the eleventh century, in one of the writings of
the poet and religious philosopher Solomon Ibn Gabirol,[1]
but it did not come into general use before the 14th century.
Of the various interpretations which have been assigned
to the word only two deserve serious notice. One is
" tradition ", implying that the mystic lore is the true
interpretation of the Torah, handed down orally. The
other is " acceptance " ; this has been suggested by David
Neumark on the basis of a passage in the book Bahir,[2]
where the mystics are spoken of as " accepted before God "
(mekubbalim lifne ha-shem מקבלים לפני השם). In fact the
mystics were later actually called " mekubbalim ", and it
is therefore conceivable that at some point the two interpretations were fused together. Apart from this, the first
interpretation itself, if we assign the origin of the tradition
to God, contains the mystical idea of a spiritual " acceptance ".

The beginnings of the Cabbalah are inseparably bound
up with an ancient Jewish secret doctrine which had already
existed previously under various designations, and of
which we have tried to give a picture in the preceding
chapters. We will now survey the further development of
this doctrine up to the appearance of the medieval Cabbalah
properly so called.

The first point we have to determine in this connection
is whether the Cabbalah is, as maintained by Graetz, in
its origin non-Jewish, and the extent to which Jewish thought,
in developing the Cabbalah, was swayed by non-Jewish
influences.

From what has been said in the first chapter on the
mystical element in the Bible—to which too little attention
has hitherto been paid in investigations into the history
of the Cabbalah—it is evident that the answer to the first

of these questions is in the negative. It is true that in style and character the secret lore contained in the Bible[3] bears little resemblance to that of later times. But, as Joel points out, the Bible in many places[4] speaks of the priests as teachers ; and when Malachi says that " the teaching of truth was in the mouths of the priests " (II, 6), he was probably referring to something more than mere ritual law, while the existence of " schools of the prophets " is a proof of the deliberate cultivation of prophetic faculties.[5]

It is also worthy of note that the period of the Babylonian captivity coincides with a turning-point in the general religious history of mankind. It was almost at this time that Pythagoras lived in Babylon and received there the teachings of Nazaratas, who was designated by Greek tradition as the renewer of the old Zarathustra teaching or as a younger Zarathustra. The same epoch also witnessed the appearance at opposite ends of the earth of such important religious figures as the Roman king Numa Pompilius, the adept of the Etruscan mysteries, the Indian king's son Gautama, who as Buddha traversed the distant East, and the Chinese sage Confucius.

The earliest mention of a Jewish secret doctrine is in the well known warning in the Book of Sirach, III, 20-24 :

> Neither search the things that are above thy strength,
> But what is commanded thee, think thereon with reverence.
> For it is not needful for thee to see with thine eyes the things that are in secret.
> Be not curious in unnecessary matters ;
> For more things are showed unto thee than men understand.

A slightly different version of the same passage is quoted in the passage referring to the secret teaching in the Talmud tractate Chagigah : " Seek not things that are too hard for thee and search not things that are hidden from thee. The things that have been permitted thee, think thereupon ; thou hast no business with the things that are secret." Later legends connect Ben Sira with the prophet Jeremiah on one side and with the Sefer Yezirah on the other. Thus we read in the Sefer ha-Gematria of Jehudah ha-Chassid : " Ben Sira wanted to study the Sefer Yezirah when an heavenly voice came out and said, ' Thou canst not do it alone '. So he went to his father Jeremiah . . . and they studied it. At the end of three years a man was created by them, on whose forehead was written ' Emet ' (truth), as on the forehead of Adam. Then the one whom they had created said to them : ' God created Adam, and when He wanted to put him to death He erased a letter from the word *emet* and it became *met* (dead). So much the more reason is there why I should want to do the same, so that you may not again create a man and the world go astray through him like the generation of Enosh . . .' "

Similarly in Yalkut Reubeni : " Jeremiah began to study the Sefer Yezirah, when a heavenly voice came forth and said : ' Get thee an associate.' He accordingly went to his son Sira, and they studied the Sefer Yezirah together. Finally . . . a man was created by them, upon whose forehead was written ' *emet* '. The person created had a knife in his hand and was erasing the letter *aleph* of the word *emet* . . ."[6]

Mordell suggests that the old Jewish number and letter mysticism, and especially the Sefer Yezirah, can be traced back to the Pythagoreans, or even to Pythagoras himself. There are certainly resemblances between the older Pythagorean school and the old Jewish secret doctrine, but there are also marked differences. There is nothing in the latter— if we except the Pythagorean Philo—of the symbolical interpretation of the numbers as such which is customary among the Pythagoreans ; a specific virtue of numbers, according to it, is to be seen solely in the arrangements and sum totals, though to be sure these are of capital importance in the Sefer Yezirah. On the other hand the letter-mysticism is quite strange to the older Pythagoreans, and came into Greek thought only through oriental, gnostic and Jewish influence.[7]

Many scholars have sought to connect the Sefer Yezirah and the early development of the Cabbalah in general with the so-called Gnosis. Grætz[8] for instance held that the teaching of the Sefer Yezirah in respect of method follows the number and letter mysticism of Marcus and the Valentinian Gnostics, while in respect of its subject matter it derives from the doctrine of emanations and syzygies[9] found in the writings of the pseudo-Clementines. With regard to letters and numbers, however, it may be remarked that the close connection of this method with the Hebrew language and with the mysteries of the Hebrew name of God is evidence of the original character of this side of the Jewish secret lore. The other Gnostic teachings which are cited belong to a stream of oriental thought which embraced much more than the teaching of the Greek-Syrian gnosis. And we must not overlook the significance of the Jewish sects for the Greek and Christian, as also for the anti-Christian Gnosis.[10] In any case this connection has been exaggerated, and its importance is probably not very great for the development of Jewish mysticism. The scope of the Gnostic teaching itself—which contained Persian, Babylonian, Egyptian, Greek, and Jewish elements fused together—is difficult to determine, since the greater part of the relevant literature has been destroyed by the Roman Church, and the content of the teaching itself has been much distorted in the accounts of the hostile Church Fathers.[11] A decisive ground for rejecting such a connection is, on the one hand, the close relation of the Gnosis to the infant Christianity, and on the other hand the violent hostility displayed by many of the older Gnostic sects to the Jewish tradition, even to the fundamental tenets of the Jewish God-idea and moral law, as when, for instance, the Cainites and the Ophites[12] made Cain or the serpent-seducer the object of particular veneration, or when the adherents of Marcion turned the Creator of this evil world into an evil being under the name of Jaldabaot, etc. It is probable, however, that there were relations between Jewish mysticism and the contemporary gnosis in Egypt, Syria, etc., especially in view of the fact that the period when the pure gnosis (Basilides, Valentinus) was flourishing—the second century of the Christian era—practically coincides with the date of the scanty records of the Talmudic secret teaching.

In the matter of doctrine there are not a few points of contact between Cabbalah and Gnosis. Such are the special importance attached to light and its emanations, the Gnostic doctrine of the æons, which perhaps correspond to the sefiroth, and of the syzygies (v. supra), and the letter-mysticism which appears in the Gnosis, though perhaps occupying only a secondary place there. Quite in the spirit of the Cabbalah, and especially of the Zohar, is the distinction drawn between a " visible " and a " concealed " fire, or the designation by Basilides of " Not-being " as the Creator of the Universe, or the reference by the same author to a " seed " of the universe.

A close examination of the Sefer Yezirah[13] reveals clearly old Persian influences. The arrangement of the " ten Sefiroth " in such a way as to make space spring from good and evil and these from time (the abyss of the beginning and the abyss of the end, I, 5) seems to have its prototype in the Persian doctrine that out of " boundless time " sprang the opposition of good and evil (Ormuzd and Ahriman), and space in turn was generated from these. Also the seven Powers, in part mere abstract qualities, in part real beings, which correspond to the seven planets seem to have their prototype in the seven Persian Amesha-spentas[14] (divine powers with Ormuzd at their head). This idea is rendered more probable by the fact that a similar group of seven is directly attributed by Plutarch to[15] the Persians ; according to a modern scholar, Joseph Pascher,[16] it reappears in Philo in the form of divine primordial powers.

Ad. Kohut[17] has shown that the Hebrew names of the angels and demons in the talmud are often derived from the Persians ; we have already mentioned that the name Metatron is by many connected with Mithras.[18] A Mithras liturgy published by Dieterich is said to show many parallels with the Hechaloth mysticism.[19]

Leo Baeck[20] has sought to trace back the Cabbalah, and especially the Cabbalistic doctrine of emanations, to the Neo-Platonist Proclus. The truth is, however, that the doctrine of emanations is much older than neo-Platonism, already making its appearance in Parseeism and in other oriental religious systems. Still it is worthy of note that in Judaism the doctrine of emanations,[21] as well as other basic ideas of Gnosticism, is not found fully elaborated till we come to the medieval Cabbalah, in particular the Zohar.

To gain a proper view of the development of the Jewish mystic lore, we must also consider its geographical dissemination. Without doubt its original centre was in the Holy Land. The supposition of Weinstein that it came to Palestine from Alexandria along with the Agada and the allegorical exegesis, and so represents the same trend of thought as Philo, is disproved by the fact that the mystic teachings with regard to the creation, the Merkabah, and the Name of God, are in direct line with the Bible, and also by the intimate connection of this teaching with the Hebrew language, of which Philo knew so little. The opposite is true, that important elements of the mystic tradition enriched Alexandrinian thought, though from Alexandria they seem to have found their way back to Palestine with accretions from Greek thought.

The subsequent gradual transference of the centre of Judaism and of Jewish learning to Mesopotamia naturally carried with it the mystic tradition also. In the tractate Chagigah (13a)[22] the Academy of Pumbeditha is specified as one of the places where this tradition was cultivated, and among its representatives the names of both Palestinian and Babylonian scholars are mentioned.[23]

In the ninth century the knowledge of Jewish mysticism, which hitherto had been confined to the Orient, was for the first time carried from Bagdad to Europe. This was an important turning-point in the history of the Cabbalah, and is connected by a half-legendary tradition with the name of Aaron of Bagdad (Ahron ha-Babli).

The study of mysticism was carried along with that of the Talmud into new regions by the distinguished family of the Kalonymides, which first settled in Lucca (Kalonymus of Lucca) and from there emigrated to the Rhineland, where it was granted special privileges, and where it produced the founders of the so-called " German " Chassidism. Even before this, Jewish mysticism must have been known in Italy,[24] since already in the tenth century Sabbatai Donolo composed in that country a commentary on the Sefer Yezirah, and synagogue poems appeared which showed the influence of the Merkabah lore. Still more noteworthy is the penetration of mystical elements from the Orient even into the later Cabbalah, as this affords proof of the essential unity of the mystic doctrine in spite of great differences of time and place.[25] In its European surroundings the Cabbalah did not at first materially change its character, though gradually it began to exhibit traces of the influence of European, i.e., Spanish, Provençal and German non-Jewish mysticism.[26]

The Cabbalah which now began to be disseminated, though it contained superstitious elements, was far from being a mere superstition, as it has often been described. On the other hand, Moses Gaster[27] went too far in proclaiming it to be a comprehensive philosophical system. This is in so far correct that the Cabbalah does indeed deal with the great matters which are the subject of the " ultimate questionings ". But its method is totally different from that of any system of philosophy, even the Jewish religious philosophy. Perhaps the best way to grasp its peculiar nature is to regard it as a combination of philosophy, mysticism, and tradition, all fused into one.

The representatives of the mystic lore received designations which varied in different ages. Thus they were known at different times as *Yod'e chen* (" Those who know the Grace of God," *v.* p. 49) ; *Ba'ale ha-Sod* (" Bearers of the Secret ") ; *Chachme ha-Tushiah* (" Students of profound knowledge," Ibn Ezra) ; *Yod'im* (" Gnostics," Nachmanides); and *Anshe maaseh* (" Men of Action," the Lucian mystics).

It goes without saying that the records which have been preserved give only an incomplete picture of the rise of the Cabbalah, and most of its early teaching is buried in obscurity. The result is that we find it difficult to account for the sudden appearance of certain teachings or literary documents, which seem to have little connection with what went before. This applies especially to the most important work of the Cabbalah, the Zohar, which emerged towards the end of the 13th century.

NOTES TO CHAPTER IV.

[1] M. H. Landauer points out in " Literaturblatt des Orients " (1845) that the actual term הקבלה חכמת (Wisdom of the Cabbalah) is first found in Gabirol's work *Tikkun Middoth Ha-Nefesh.*

[2] *V.* Book Bahir, 46.

[3] Abelson distinguishes between the mysticism of the Bible and the mystical doctrine which first appeared later.

[4] Deut. XXXIII, 10; Mal. II, 6 and 7.   *V.* Joel, Die Religionsphilosophie des Sohar," p. 18.

[5] *V.* ch. I.

[6] Transcribed from P. Mordell, " The Origin of Letters and Numbers, according to the Sepher Yezirah " (*v.* Index).

[7] The opposite view, that the Greek letter-mysticism was earlier, is maintained by Franz Dornseiff in his work " Das Alphabet in Mystik und Magie ". *Cf.* also O. Fischer, " Orientalische und griechische Zahlensymbolik ".

[8] In " Gnosticismus und Judentum ", 1846.

[9] In the Gnosis, syzygies denote pairs of cosmically polar opposites. *V.* G. R. S. Mead, " Fragments of a faith forgotten ".

[10] This has been well brought out by Moritz Friedländer in his " Der vorchristliche jüdische Gnosticismus " (1898), and in subsequent investigations on the same subject (*v.* Index).   An interesting parallel between the Gnosis and the early Cabbalah is found in a passage in the " Pistis Sophia ", the Gnostic gospel, where Jesus before the birth of John the Baptist is said to bind the power of the "lesser YAV" (= YHWH, *v.* p. 53) and the soul of Elijah with the body of John. *V.* Mead's edition, p. 12.

[11] The Gnosis is adversely commented upon by Irenaeus in his " Refutationes ", by Origen in his " Contra Celsum ", and by Hippolytus. Polemics against it by Justin Martyr and others have been lost.   Clement of Alexandria also speaks of the Gnostics in various works.   The chief modern accounts are those of Mead, and King, Scholz and Leisegang (*v.* Index).

[12] The Ophites, however, corresponded to a Jewish-Gnostic sect, the Nachashites (from נחש, serpent). To the more reputable Jewish-Gnostic sects belonged the Ebionites and the Melchizedekites described by Paul (in the Epistle to the Hebrews, ch. V and VII).

[13] V. the author's essay on the Sefer Yezirah in " Mezudah " (London, 1943).

[14] Lit. " Holy Watchers ", v. p. 59. The seven Powers mentioned in the Sefer Yezirah (IV, 1) are Life, Peace, Wisdom, Riches, Beauty, Fertility, and Domination. The opposites are Death, War, Folly, Poverty, Ugliness, Desolation, Servitude.

[15] In " De Iside et Osiride ", ch. 47.

[16] In his treatise, " Der Königsweg der Vergottung und Wiedergeburt bei Philon von Alexandria ", especially the chapter, " Die Mysterienlehre über den Ewigen und seine Kräfte ".

[17] In his book, " Die jüdische Angelologie und Dämonologie in ihrer Abhängigkeit vom Parsismus ".

[18] V. p. 54. There are also Persian prototypes for the good and evil inclination.

[19] V. Sholem, p. 360.

[20] In " Zum Sepher Jezirah " and " Die Zehn Sephiroth im Sepher Jezirah." V. Index.

[21] See for example Marcus Ehrenpreis, " Die Entwicklung der Emanationslehre in der Kabbala des XIII Jahrhunderts ", Frankfurt a. M., 1895.

[22] Which contains such statements as " R. Joseph was studying the work of the Chariot " . . . " The Elders of Pumbeditha were studying the work of the Chariot." One of the earliest Babylonian mystics is the R. Abba so frequently mentioned in the Zohar as a disciple of R. Simeon b. Yochai.

[23] V. Sholem, p. 40. Babylonia was also perhaps the headquarters of the " Yorde Merkabah " (v. supra), and there too the most prominent of the Geonim, Saadiah and Hai, at least wrote on the Cabbalah, if they did not follow its practices.

[24] V. Sholem, p. 83.

[25] Eleazar of Worms traces the tradition back to Babylon as follows. He himself learnt Cabbalistic mysteries from R. Judah ha-Chassid; R. Judah from his father R. Samuel ha-Chassid; R. Samuel from R. Eleazar Chazan of Speyer; R. Eleazar from R. Kalonymus of Lucca; R. Kalonymus from his father R. Isaac; R. Isaac from his father R. Eleazar ha-Gadol; and R. Eleazar of R. Simeon ha-Gadol, the line of whose teachers went back to R. Moses the Elder, the son of R. Samuel ha-Nasi, who had to leave Babylon. (V. Jellinek, " Auswahl kabbalistischer Mystik," pp. 11–12.) A later Cabbalistic influx is indicated by a statement of R. Shemtob (quoted by Jellinek) that R. Kashisha, who had come from Sura to Apulia, there gave Cabbalistic instruction to R. Judah ha-Chassid, who had hastened to him from Corbeil, and composed a Cabbalistic compendium for him.

[26] V. ch. IX.

[27] " The Origin of the Kabbala." V. Index.

V

CABBALAH IN EUROPE

In tracing the history of the Cabbalah in Europe in the eleventh, twelfth and thirteenth centuries, we find—as we should expect in dealing with a secret doctrine—on the one hand a large number of anonymous writings on the subject, on the other hand the names of numerous Cabbalistic personages mentioned with high respect, without such indications as would enable us to refer the works and the authors to one another with any certainty. Among the writings from this period which have come down to us without the name of any author, or which are attributed to certain talmudical personages, or the authorship of which can be conjectured more or less plausibly, the following may be mentioned : the "Tractate of the Emanation" (*Masecheth Aziluth*), the treatise *Ma'arecheth Elohuth* (God's Ordering of the World), a commentary on the Ten Sefiroth (*Perush 'Eser Sefiroth*), the treatise *Keter Shem Tob* (Crown of a Good Name),[1] the *Sefer ha-Emunah we-ha-Bittachon* (Book of Faith and Trust), the Book Raziel, the *Sefer Temunah* (Book of the Likeness), and the *Sefer ha-Bahir* (Book of Brightness), which is the most akin to the Zohar.[2]

The mystical Cabbalistic schools and tendencies of this epoch have their centre first in Germany, then in South France, especially Provence, and finally in Spain, from where they made their way once more to Italy.

In Germany, where Jews had been settled for centuries, especially in the Rhineland and Franconia, there sprang from the family of the Kalonymides, in addition to prominent Talmudists, the Cabbalists Samuel ha-Chassid (the Pious), his son Judah ha-Chassid from Regensburg, and the latter's disciple Eleazar ben Judah of Worms, known also as Rokeach, after his principal work ; among his disciples the most prominent was Abraham from Cologne. The central figure among all these is Judah ha-Chassid,[3] who became the subject of many legends, and to whom was attributed the *Sefer Chassidim* (Book of the Pious), a work of popular character which exercised a wide influence. The name Chassid, which first appears in the Psalms with the meaning of " pious ". was applied in the time of the Maccabees to those Jews who most steadfastly resisted the Hellenising tendencies of the day ; and no doubt Judah was regarded by himself and his contemporaries as their spiritual descendant.

The " German Chassidism " inaugurated by the Sefer Chassidim anticipated, in some ways, the popular religious movement of the same name founded by Israel Baalshem in Eastern Europe in the eighteenth century. Like this, it made its chief goal the cultivation of inner piety, with which it combined a mystical attitude towards prayer and the letter and sound elements of the " holy Name ". This cultivation of inner piety and constant sense of God's presence as the goal to be aimed at constituted a new phase in Jewish mysticism ; the older secret lore had striven to bring the adept nearer to God through the training of the ecstatic-visionary faculties, or at least, where this could not be attained, through the exploration of celestial mysteries. It is here too that we find the origin of certain ideas which, tending as they do to intensify religious practice, became very popular in modern Chassidism, such as that of " Devekuth ", or the " clinging " to God, or of " Yichud ", the intuitive grasping of the divine unity. On the other side the highest importance is attached to asceticism and penitence, if not as ends in themselves, at any rate as preparations, as in the Merkabah mysticism. Above all, however, a distinctive character is given in these circles to prayer, which becomes a kind of meditation, equally removed from the formalism of the talmudic prescriptions and from the essentially selfish magical tendencies of the incantation mysticism. Only as the crown of the pious life did the Cabbalist indulge in study of the holy names of God or speculation on the " Kabod ", the personified divine majesty. It was natural therefore that Judah or

Samuel ha-Chassid should be regarded as the author of the two great liturgical hymns, *Shir ha-Yichud* (hymn of unity) and *Shir ha-Kabod* (Song of Divine Majesty).[4]

The fundamental outlook of this Chassidism is revealed in the opening words of the Massecheth Aziluth, which was apparently the product of another circle of mystics[5] :

"Eliahu ben Joseph began with the text, '*The secret of the Lord is with them that fear Him*' (Ps. XXV, 14). What do we learn here if not that the Holy One, blessed be He, discloses His secret to none save them that fear Him ? If an Israelite has studied Torah, Mishnah, Gemara and Tosefta,[6] but possesses no reverence, then it is a useless endeavour for him 'to plunge into the mighty waters', and however much he may labour, it is in vain. But he who fears God may seek for the secrets and the Maaseh Merkabah, which forms the very essence of wisdom and knowledge, and of which it is said : *The fear of the Lord is the beginning of wisdom* " (Ps. CXI, 10). An iron breast-plate, a steel sword is the fear of God, having which a man need be afraid of nothing. For so it says, "*The sinners in Israel are afraid*" (Is. XXXIII, 14), implying that he who avoids sin has nothing to fear, since the Shechinah stands before him[7] and protects him, and in consequence the hidden secrets are revealed to him. To this refer the words, "*The fear of the Lord is the beginning of wisdom*". Also the words : "*Behold, the fear of the Lord, that is wisdom, and to depart from evil is understanding*" (Job, XXVIII, 28).

Eleazar of Worms[8] in his main work *Rokeach* (Lit. "apothecary") also expounds a mysticism applied first and foremost to ethical conduct, and embracing all branches of the religious and ceremonial life. This book is one of the first examples of a tendency which sought to combine strict adherence to the Rabbinic law with cabbalistic mysticism. So we find that on the one hand numerous cabbalistic writings—mostly preserved only in manuscript, like *Sode Raza* (mystic secrets)—are attributed to Eleazar of Worms, while on the other hand he composed commentaries to talmudic tractates. He also wrote exegetical notes on the

Bible, commentaries on the prayers, and liturgical poems, especially penitential hymns.

Abraham of Cologne was, according to a statement of Solomon ben Adreth, eminent as a preacher, and is in some places mentioned as author of the *Keter Shem Tob* (*v. supra*), which has been edited by Adolf Jellinek and deals with the Tetragrammaton. Only slightly later is the cabbalistic school of Provence, to which belonged Jacob ha-Nazir, Abraham ben Isaac, and his son-in-law, Abraham ben David from Posquières. The last-named is the reputed author of an important commentary on the Sefer Yezirah which has been preserved ; Sholem, however, assigns it to another author, Joseph ben Shalom Ashkenazi (15th century). The most prominent representative of this school is the son of Abraham, Isaac, known as *Sagi-nahor* (lit., " very clear-sighted ", in the spiritual sense, but also a euphemism for " blind "), whom legend regarded as a saint, and later repeatedly designated as " Father of the Cabbalah ".[9] Landauer and Jellinek consider him to be the author of the book Bahir, in the opening words of which, with reference to certain verses in the Psalms, the inner light is opposed to the external darkness. Isaac is said to have laid special stress on the doctrine of the transmigration of souls ; and in fact it seems that in this circle particular attention was given to the study of the soul. Later representatives of this school are the nephew of Isaac, Asher ben David, and his disciples Azriel and Ezra ben Solomon.[10] Azriel designates the Cabbalah *Chokhmath ha-Ani* (" Wisdom of the Ego "). For the external history of the Cabbalah he is of importance because he transplanted the Cabbalah from France to Spain, and with his commentary on the Song of Songs exercised a great influence on the great biblical exegete Moses ben Nachman (Nachmanides).

In Spain the Cabbalah assumed a more philosophical form, due to the influence of the religious philosophy which was already fully developed in that country. There are numerous points of contact between it and the work of the three great thinkers Jehudah Halevi, Solomon Ibn Gabirol, and Abrahan Ibn Ezra. The first-named devoted some space to the Sefer Yezirah in his great work Cuzari. Gabirol as a neo-Platonist has many resemblances with the Cabbalah ; these have been pointed out by Isaac Myer in his book *Qabbalah*, and before him also by Stössel. In particular the idea of a freely creating Primordial Will as the ultimate source of being seems to have found its way from him into the Cabbalah. His doctrine with regard to the soul also has an echo in the Zohar. Mystical observations occur in many of his poems, above all in the cosmological hymn *Kether Malchuth* (Crown of Majesty), the title of which is reminiscent of the close connection taught in the Cabbalah between the highest and the lowest of the Sefiroth (" Kether " and " Malchuth "), and which itself describes the spiritual Cosmos in the framework of the planetary spheres.

Finally Abraham Ibn Ezra made mystical numeral and literal analyses of the Name of God, particularly in his writings *Yesod Mora* (" Basis of the Fear of God "), *Zachuth* (" Clearness "), *Moznayim* (" Balance "), *Sefer-ha-Shem* (" Book of the Name "), *Sefer ha-Mispar* (" Book of Number "), and *Sefer ha-Echad* (" Book of Unity "), frequently repeating himself verbally. Similar observations are scattered throughout his commentary on the Pentateuch, often accompanied by the remark, " the initiated will understand ". In these researches cabbalistic, Pythagorean, grammatical and mathematical ideas are intertwined. Many of the calculations are again found in the work *Kether Shem Tob.*

The great Jewish religious philosopher Moses Maimonides (1135—1204), whose rationalism did not prevent him from believing in the existence of angels and in the reality of prophecy, speaks of the " secrets of the Torah " (*v.* p. 42 *supra*) in the 71st chapter of his great work "The Guide of the Perplexed " (*Moreh Nebuchim*), and says that they are transmitted only by a chosen few to a chosen few, and that this was the reason which inevitably led to these essential doctrines disappearing from the popular creed ;

it also explains why there are only a few insignificant references to them in the Talmud and Midrash. These resemble small kernels wrapped round in numerous outer husks, so that people occupy themselves only with the husks and have no idea that any inner kernel is hidden within them.

A man who was described as having one foot in philosophy and the other in Cabbalah was Isaac ben Abraham Ibn Latif[11] (Arabic *Allatif*) who composed among other works the books *Rav Po'olim* ("Abundant in Works"), *Zurath ha-Olam* ("Form of the World"), *Zeror ha-Mor* ("Bundle of Myrrh"), and commentaries to the biblical books Job and Ecclesiastes. Isaac ibn Latif lays special stress on the doctrine of the *creatio ex nihilo*, and identifies the Creator of the Universe with an absolutely free Primordial Will (*Chefetz* or *Ratzon*). Between God and the world there must be intermediate beings, of whom the highest is designated the First Created (*Nibra ha-Rishon*), from whom the other "abstract intelligences" spring by way of emanation. To explain the process of emanation itself Ibn Latif employs mathematical conceptions, comparing it to the formation of the dimensions of space from the point and of numbers from unity. By these methods, and with the assistance of the Aristotelian concepts of matter and form, he endeavours to explain the grades of the angelic and planetary worlds, as also of the Sefiroth.

One of the most notable personalities of this whole period is the Cabbalist Abraham ben Samuel Abulafia, who regarded both philosophy and Cabbalah as merely preparatory steps to a "prophetical Cabbalah" (*Kabbalah nebuith*), which was to be a distinct stage, and which he himself claimed to represent. The root of this idea was to be found in the teaching of Maimonides regarding prophecy, and it was to be realised through the investigation of the names of God, which would ultimately lead to the exercise of magical powers, to be preceded of course by the proper purification of the soul. A responsum and a small treatise of Abulafia, entitled *Sefer ha-Oth* ("Book of the Sign, or the Letter ")[12] have been published by Jellinek, and more recently numerous manuscripts of Abulafia's writings have been discovered. On the strength of these Scholem regards his system as the most important product of the medieval Cabbalah next to the Zohar. In his book "Major Trends of Jewish Mysticism", Sholem cites, along with a number of passages from Abulafia's works in an English translation,[13] a report of one of his disciples which analyses with great psychological subtlety the difference in character between philosophical thought and the mystical path. He describes this path minutely along with its external pre-requisites; it includes a progressive liberation not only from sense impressions, but also from extraneous intellectual interests. The disciple absorbs himself in the "letters" until he feels the inspiration streaming in upon him. His unnamed cabbalistic teacher—perhaps Abulafia himself—addresses him as follows with regard to this "path of the Names": "The less understandable they are, the higher their order until you arrive at the activity of a force which is no longer in your control, but rather your reason and your thought is in its control" (p. 147).

Abulafia worked out these doctrines in the course of an unsettled, not to say, adventurous life. Born in 1240 in Saragossa, at the age of eighteen he migrated to the Holy Land, and later took up his residence successively in Spain, Greece and Italy. On the day before the New Year holy day in 1280 he sought to convert Pope Nicholas III to Judaism, and narrowly escaped the scaffold for his temerity. He is said after that to have appeared in Sicily as a wonder-worker and Messiah. He died in 1291. In Abraham Abulafia we can discern a bold and independent thinker on mystical lines; but also perhaps a forerunner of that visionary and delusive Messianism which later led David Reubeni and Solomon Molcho, Sabbatai Zevi and Jacob Frank into such strange, and in the case of the two latter, even dangerous courses.

The example set by Abulafia of close study of the names of God exercised a strong influence on many of his successors,

notably on Joseph ben Abraham ibn Gikatilla, who lived
in Castile from 1248 to 1305. In his two chief works *Ginath
Egoz*[14] (" Garden of Nuts ") and *Sha'are Orah* (" Gates of
Light "), which later was translated into Latin, he weaves
the doctrine of the names of God into an elaborate system.
He follows Ibn Ezra in grouping the divine appellations
around the two central four-lettered names Ehyeh
(אהיה) and Jehovah (יהוה), the former of which constitutes the root and the latter the trunk of the tree. There
are in addition ten further designations taken from the
Bible, which correspond to the ten Sefiroth, and, organically
connected with these, there are further numerous designations of divine attributes which serve as secondary divine
names. So, in the words of Gikatilla, the " name YHWH
clothes itself with the other denominations of God ". In
his *Sefer ha-Nikkud* (" Book of Punctuation ") Gikatilla
extends the mystical treatment of the letters to the vowel
signs. Other works of his, preserved only in manuscript,
include a commentary on Maimonides, a treatise, *Sod ha-
Chashmal* (" Secret of the Chashmal ")[15] belonging to the
Merkabah mysticism, and also mystical interpretations of
religious practices, such as later became more and more
frequent in cabbalistic literature, and a commentary on the
Passover Haggadah.

With the names of Moses ben Shemtob de Leon (of whom
more will be said in the next chapter), Isaac of Acre, and
Moses ben Nachman (Nachmanides),[16] the biblical commentator, we come to writers who are linked either historically or by legend with the Zohar. The last-named is said to
have been introduced to the Cabbalah by Judah ibn Jakar,
Azriel and Ezra, and he gives it a place in his celebrated
commentary on the Pentateuch. In the introduction, after
expressing his belief that the Torah was transcribed by
Moses from the divinely created original, he makes the
following significant remarks : " We have a well attested
tradition (*kabbalah shel emeth*) that the whole Torah consists of names of God, since the syllables are capable of
being divided according to the names, as, for instance, the

words *bereshith bara* may be so divided as to read,
'berosh yithbare' (בראש יתברא=בראשיתברא); this quite
apart from the combinations of letters (*zerufim*) and
their numerical values (*gematriot*) . . . It would seem that
the Torah, which is written with black fire on white fire,
has been put together without any division of syllables,
so that it is possible to read it either according to the method
of the names or the method of subject and precept. In
this way it was given to Moses, namely, to pick out the
precepts. On the other hand the method of reading it
according to the names was transmitted to him orally."
Moses b. Nachman also wrote a commentary to the Song
of Songs, which contains extracts from the commentary
of Azriel.

From the account which has been given above of the
main trends of the Cabbalah in this epoch, it will not be
difficult to understand why it has been usual since about
the 13th century to make a distinction between the
"theoretical" or strictly "contemplative" Cabbalah
(*Kabbalah 'Iyunith*)[17], and the "practical Cabbalah"
(*Kabbalah Ma'asiyith*). This latter term is used in a double
sense, applying sometimes to the inner religious activity of
the soul, sometimes to an external, magical activity. In the
former of these senses the whole of Chassidism is essentially
practical mysticism, in which the magical "use" (*Shimmush*) of the divine names, as already mentioned, is per-
missible only after the requisite purification has been
attained. The external magic on the contrary forms the
starting-point for both Jewish and non-Jewish occult side-
paths, often of a suspicious character. On the other side
the influence of philosophy gave a further impulse to the
contemplative element, which however frequently glides
from mystic intuition into speculative thought that from
a mystical point of view is often barren. The method of
mystical inquiry is determined less by the laws of formal
logic than by the special character of the subject in hand.
In this sense Abulafia, as already mentioned, speaks
of a "method of the names" (*Derech ha-Shemoth*), just

as we often hear, for example, of a "method of the Sefiroth" (*Derech ha-Sefiroth*), and also of a "method of numbers"; Abelson too designates the Merkabah a "mystical way".

The chief product of Cabbalistic thought in this epoch was, next to the doctrine of the names of God, which belongs also to the practical Cabbalah, a highly developed cosmology, embodied on the one hand in the doctrine of the Emanations, on the other in that of the Sefiroth. In the above-mentioned "Tractate of the Emanations" the outlines of these doctrines are set forth briefly and systematically. According to the doctrine of the Emanations the world has not only been created by the Godhead, but has sprung from it in stages. As the highest stage we must imagine a pure radiation, at once self-mirroring and self-reproducing, the first result of which has already met us under many designations—as Logos, Sophia, Elohim, Angel of YHWH, *Ruach Elohim*, *Makom*, *Kabod*, Metatron, *Nibra ha-Rishon* ; as first divine revelation, as first-created being, as world-creating power, or as the highest angelic being. Three further stages of emanation derive their names from the verse in Isaiah XLIII, 7 : "*That which is called by My name, I have created it* (barativ), *I have formed it* (yezartiv), *and I have also made it* (' asitiv) ". On this basis four stages of creation, and with them four worlds, are distinguished : the World of Emanation (*Olam ha-Aziluth*), the World of Creation, in the narrower sense (*Olam ha-Beriah*), the World of Formation (*Olam ha-Yezirah*), and the World of Action or Making (*Olam ha-Asiyah*). The creation described in the Book of Genesis corresponds to the second stage. Only in the third stage is the world fashioned with measure, number and form. The fact that the Sefer Yezirah deals obviously with the third stage affords a proof that the distinction of the four stages is much older than the actual medieval doctrine of the emanations.[18] Not before the fourth stage do we reach the work of the physical world, in which man also has a creative share. That this work is to be continued after that described in the biblical account of the creation is indicated by the concluding word of that account, " in order to do " (*la'asoth*), i.e., to carry on the work.

According to the arrangement of the *Masecheth Aziluth*, the World of Emanation is the seat of the Shechinah. In the World of Creation the souls of the righteous have their origin, and here too are to be found the treasures of blessing and life, the divine Throne, and the seven Hechaloth, including the Sapphire Heaven as the foundation of the world. The " World of Formation " contains the four creatures of the vision of Ezekiel, the ministering angels and the ten angelic hierarchies which preside over the Sefiroth, led by Metatron, " who was transformed from flesh and blood into fire " ; also the spirits of human beings and various creatures connected with the " Chariot ". Finally the " World of Making " contains the Ofanim and those angels which deal with prayers and the will of men, and those which, led by the angel Sandalphon, carry on a combat with Samael and the world of evil.

The Sefiroth—a term which has gone through many meanings—are designated in the Tractate qualities and instruments of God, and the name is brought into connection with the " Sapphire Heaven " (Exodus XXIV, 10). In the names which it gives to the Sefiroth, in their arrangement in ten angelic hierarchies, and in their identification with certain biblical characters understood symbolically, this treatise contains the germ of a doctrine which, after going through many preliminary stages, reached its full development in the Zohar. Also the idea that the Deity through the self-concentration of light (*Zimzum*) created room for darkness and for multiplicity forms the germ of a doctrine which was not fully developed till much later.[19]

In the " Commentary on the Ten Sefiroth " and in the treatise *Maarecheth Elohuth* cabbalistic cosmology is based on philosophical grounds. At the period when these works were composed there were several opposing views with regard to the creation of the world : the Aristotelian, which maintained the eternity of the world, the view that the world was created from nothing (represented by Ibn Gabirol and Ibn Latif), and the doctrine of Emanations. In addition there was the doctrine of the pre-existence of certain conditions mentioned in the Midrash and in the Book Bahir. Bound up with the problem of creation is that of the transcendence or immanence of the Godhead—whether it is completely dissociated from the created world or dwells in it. The character of the divine essence as absolutely immaterial, indivisible, and unalterable, seems to conflict with the possibility of a direct creation through a definite act of will. Such a theory therefore postulates the existence of intermediate beings (angels) and intermediate worlds between the original divine being and the phenomenal world, and these are constituted by the Sefiroth. It appeared, however, to be an infringement of monotheism when the Sefiroth were regarded as divine radiations, and were even made the object of prayers like the angels. Hence they were again regarded as mere appearances which, like the divine attributes of the religious philosophy, represented not the Godhead itself but its revelation to men or its adaptation to men's capacity to understand.

The book Temunah (" Form ") also concerns itself with the problem of the Sefiroth, which according to it belong as immediately to the Godhead as the limbs to the human organism, being like them united through a common will which is active in them. The book takes its name from the form of the Hebrew letters, which are used to illustrate the various grades of emanation. The book Temunah further assumes a double series of emanations, adding to the seven upper, positive Sefiroth seven negative ones as the basis of evil. The Zohar, however, is the first Cabbalistic work which makes comprehensive attempts to solve the problem of evil, drawing to some extent on the Midrash literature for this purpose.

The book Raziel stands poles apart both from the intuitive and from the philosophical trend of the Cabbalah. After a legendary account of the way in which an angel

made the patriarchs, from Adam to Noah, acquainted with
the mysteries, it deals with the use of the names of God
and of mystical letter-formulæ for magical purposes, and
describes and even gives drawings of amulets of various
kinds.

NOTES TO CHAPTER V

[1] Shem tob is the designation of the beneficent Name of God (*cf.*
pp. 137–139).

[2] Two kindred works of a somewhat later time (14th century) are the
" Sefer ha-Kanah " (perhaps = " Book of the Measuring Rod ") and
the " Sefer ha-Peliah " (" Book of Wonder ") both by the same author,
who calls himself, in one place, Kana ibn-Gdor, and in another, Elkana
ben Jeroboam, and who claims to be a descendant of Nechuniah ben
ha-Kaneh (*v.*, p. 45). The origin of the books is ascribed to wonderful
revelations from the prophet Elijah. One book contains an explanation
of the 248 biblical precepts on cabbalistic lines, and from this standpoint
seeks to reconcile differences between the Bible and the Talmud: the
other combats legalistic formalism in religion.

[3] To be distinguished from the mystic of the same name who lived at
the end of the 17th century : *v.* ch. VIII.

[4] Judah ha-Chassid is also said to have composed a " Sefer ha-Kabod ".
The term " kabod " is a favourite one in the religious philosophy of
Saadiah. On " Kabod " in the Bible, *v. supra,* ch. I.

[5] *V.* Jellinek, " Auswahl kabbalistischer Mystik ", IV.

[6] The name given to certain supplements to the Talmud.

[7] The translation here follows a slight correction of the meaningless
Hebrew text.

[8] Eleazar b. Judah, b. 1176 in Speyer, d. 1238 in Worms, was a victim
of misfortune, his family being murdered by the Crusaders. He is said
to have enlarged and revised the " Book of the Pious ". He was highly
esteemed as a Rabbi and helped to draw up the regulations for the three
communities of Speyer, Worms, and Mainz.

[9] E.g., by the biblical commentator Bachya ben Asher. Joseph ibn
Gikatilla and others also designate him as the founder of the Cabbalah
(*v.* Ehrenpreis, p. 20).

[10] It has been established by H. Brody that Azriel and Ezra, who
formerly were often held to be identical, were brothers.

[11] Isaac ben Abraham ibn Latif probably came from Toledo. He died
in 1290 in Jerusalem.

[12] *V.* Jellinek, " Beiträge zur Geschichte der Kabbala ", pp. 66–72,
and in the Graetz Festschrift.

[13] *V.* Sholem, " Major Trends," etc., IV. Two hymns of Abulafia
are given in an English translation in Ariel Benzion's " The Zohar in
Moslem and Christian Spain ".

[14] The word *GiNnaT* hints at the three exegetical methods of Gematria,
Notarikon, Temurah.

[15] On Chashmal, *v.* ch. II.

[16] Moses ben Nachman (Nachmanides) composed a well-known bible commentary and completed the great halachic work of Isaac Alfasi. He played a prominent part in defending Maimonides against the violent attacks of the conservative Talmudists (and also Cabbalists). After conducting a four-day religious controversy with the baptised Jew Pablo Christiani he was banished by the Pope from Aragon. At the age of seventy he migrated to the Holy Land, where he founded a synagogue and school, and where he died in Acre in 1270.

[17] It is significant that a cabbalistic work of that period, ascribed to one Chamai Gaon, bears the title " Book of Contemplation " (*Sefer ha-Iyun*). It has been published by Jellinek.

[18] *V.* Ehrenpreis, " Die Entwicklung der Emanationslehre in der Kabbala des 13. Jahrhunderts ".

[19] On this see ch. VII.

VI

THE ZOHAR

WE now come to the two central works of the Cabbalistic literature, the Zohar and its parallel on a much smaller scale, the Book Bahir.[1] There are a number of interesting resemblances between the two books. The first is in the titles. The Zohar derives its name[2] from the verse in the Book of Daniel XII, 3, " And they that be wise " (more exactly, " that affect reason ") " shall shine as the brightness (*zohar*) of the firmament ". The noun *Zohar* is found only once more in the Bible, in one of the visions of the prophet Ezekiel (VIII, 2). Similarly the adjective *Bahir*, which also denotes a certain kind of brightness, is found only in one place in the Bible, viz., Job XXXVII, 21, which is the text for the opening of the book : *And now men see not the bright light (or bahir) which is in the clouds.*

Both works were ascribed to Tannaite teachers—the Zohar to R. Simeon b. Yochai, the well known contemporary of R. Akiba, and the Book Bahir to R. Nechuniah ben Hakaneh,[3] who lived in the first century of the Christian era and was the teacher of R. Ishmael, and so may have belonged to the same mystical school. Other talmudical authorities also appear in both works as transmitters of traditions.[4] Both works are in the form of Midrash ; the Book Bahir keeps closer to the biblical texts, without, however, following the biblical order. Both of them deal with the main subjects of the Cabbalah eclectically and somewhat unsystematically. The treatment in the Zohar is broader and more homiletical, in the Book Bahir more terse and didactic. Both of them, however, show a mastery of the subject which seems to presuppose both an ancient tradition and long practice in handling it. The Book Bahir adheres closely to the main lines of the letter-mysticism, laying stress on the character of the sounds of the letters, and also, like the Book Temunah, of their shapes. In this respect it is directly related on the one hand to the Sefer

Yezirah, on the other hand to the alphabet-Midrash of
R. Akiba. The letter-mysticism is systematically developed
from paragraph 13 onwards. As in the works of Joseph ibn
Gikatilla, the vowel signs, which were introduced only
at a late period, are also interpreted mystically ; vowels
are declared " to abide in consonants like souls in
bodies " (83).[5] Some passages deal directly with difficulties
occurring in the Sefer Yezirah, as, for instance, the meaning
of the " Teli " (75 ; v. p. 49).[6] With this are connected
physiological disquisitions ; thus there is talk of the
" wisdom of the ear " (54), and the heart, brain, and marrow
are treated mystically and brought into relation with
Israel and incidentally linked up with the Festival of
Sukkoth (56, 67, 104). The ceremonies in general are treated
symbolically and mystically, above all the sacrifice, which
" brings the holy forms to one another " (62, 78). Connected with this is the mystical application of the name of
God, for instance, in the priestly blessing (80, 81), also in
the central feature of the Merkabah mysticism, the kedushah
(88). A leading place is given to subjects connected with
the creation doctrine, viz., the distinction between the
stages of Beriah and Yezirah (140), the meaning of tohu
wa-bohu (10), the relation of " heaven " to the element of
fire (68), above all, the nature of light, both the visible
light and the hidden light of the " future world " (97, 98,
106, 131). Other important passages deal with the " evil
inclination " (108, 137, 141), with the Messiah and the
future world (105, 106), with the symbolism of the Patriarchs
(131), and with reincarnation—quite a new subject (135).
The doctrine of the Sefiroth is only hinted at ; the ten
Sefiroth are denoted ten " sayings " (maamaroth)[7] ; they
seem to be regarded as related to the ten spheres, and are
assigned to certain angels (74, 77, 122). Even geometrical
symbols are found here and there (64, 83). Another
characteristic difference between the Book Bahir and the
Zohar is that the former is written in pure Hebrew, the
latter in Aramaic, or, to speak more precisely, in that
dialect of it which is peculiar to the mystical literature.

The origin of the Zohar is, like that of the Book Bahir, obscure, and the stories which have been handed down with regard to it only make it even more obscure.

The book was first published by the learned Cabbalist Mose ben Shemtob from Leon[8] as the work of Simeon b. Yochai. In contrast with this claim Abraham Zacuto at the beginning of the 15th century in his book " Sefer Yuchasin " gave the following account.[9] When the Cabbalist R. Isaac of Acre was in Spain soon after the appearance of the Zohar, he was told on inquiring into its origin that Moses ben Nachman, who was then living in Palestine, had found the manuscript of R. Simon b. Yochai and had sent it to Catalonia. From there it had been carried by a tempest to Aragon, where it had fallen into the hands of R. Moses of Leon. R. Isaac asked him to show him the original manuscript, but Moses of Leon, before he could do so, died while on the way to his home at Avila in Arevalo. After his death two rich men in Avila had promised his widow a large sum if she would show them the manuscript. The woman, however, insisted that such a document did not exist, stating that Moses de Leon had himself written the book and ascribed it to that mysterious author in order to enhance its value.[10]

Since that time the dispute regarding the authorship of the Zohar has raged continuously. Formerly the question at issue was only whether the author was Simeon b. Yochai or Moses of Leon. The former view was taken by the Cabbalists, who upheld the miraculous origin of the book, the latter by the rabbinic or philosophical rationalists who regarded it as a forgery.[11] This view was also taken by many scholars of the nineteenth century, above all by the historian Heinrich Graetz, who roundly declared the Zohar to be a clumsy forgery. It was not difficult to bring objections against ascribing a high antiquity to the book. Apart from its sudden appearance and the mysterious story of its forgery, there were features in its style and contents which seemed to conflict with the possibility of its being composed in talmudical times. Such are above all the frequent anachronisms, like the mystical interpretation of religious customs which were first introduced by medieval authorities, references to the Crusades or to the domination of Islam, and express mention of the Hebrew vowel signs. Significant too in this connection is the occurrence in the chief work of Moses of Leon of several passages which correspond word for word with passages from the Zohar. This, however, may be explained by supposing that Moses of Leon, who according to Jellinek only wrote in order to make his friends acquainted with the Cabbalah, himself copied the passages in question from the Zohar which already lay before him.

A more critical examination, however, placed the whole question of the origin of the Zohar in a new light, by showing that it is a heterogeneous composition, the parts of which belong to different dates. It was pointed out that some sections of the book are written in an archaic style which has affinities with products of the talmudic period; and these sections are sharply distinguished both from the body of the book and from later additions and supplements. To account for this fact new theories came into vogue. Adolf Franck considers some parts very ancient, containing a doctrine derived ultimately from Persia; Landauer holds that the Zohar is a work of Abraham Abulafia; Jellinek regards it as a composite work in the production of which Moses of Leon had the largest share; while Joel draws a sharp distinction between the antiquity of the teaching and the much more modern form in which it is presented. This last view has recently been energetically championed by Hillel Zeitlin,[12] who draws attention to the fact that in the literature of the period we find mention of small leaflets (" kuntressim "), in which mystical traditions were disseminated in certain circles. The rambling character of the main body of the work, the Zohar properly so called, as well as the sporadic inclusion of additional works, makes this theory highly plausible.

The text of the Zohar as we have it is actually made up as follows. The main body is in the form of a *midrash* on the weekly sections of the Torah. This is enlarged by the insertion at different places of certain small works which are much older in language and style, namely, the " Idra Rabba " (Great Assembly), the " Idra Zuta " (Lesser Assembly), and the " Sifra di Zeniutha " (Book of Secrecy), which are all closely connected with one another. The first of these books describes in high-flown language a kind of initiation scene in which R. Simeon b. Yochal takes the leading part in the midst of his disciples. Into this picture is introduced a description—similar to that in the Shiur Komah—of the anthropomorphic revelation of the Deity, to a certain extent as Adam Kadmon, with each organ separately described. The Idra Zuta relates the death of R. Simeon, and continues the anthropomorphic description. The Sifra di Zeniutha speaks in more general terms— partly with the application of letter mysticism—of the highest secrets of the divine nature. Scattered throughout the Zohar are other additions : the " Ra'ya Mehemna " (Faithful Shepherd), an ancient designation of Moses,[13] who here appears as teacher, dealing principally with the precepts and prohibitions of the Torah ; and the " Midrash ha-Neelam " (Hidden Midrash), in which along with R. Simeon appear other authorities (e.g., R. Eliezer b. Hyrcanus[14]) as teachers, and the scene seems to be fre- quently transplanted to the heavenly regions, Simeon b. Yochai, for instance, being in communication with the prophet Elijah and other mystical figures. Shorter inser- tions are the " Sitre Torah " (Secrets of the Law), on various biblical sentences, "Matnitin " and "Tosefta " (copied from the style of the Mishnah and Tosefta), and " Raza de Razin " (Secret of Secrets), physiognomical and chiro- mantic fragments. Completely embodied in the text are the " Hechaloth " (a description of the seven heavenly palaces), " Yanuka " (revelations of a child), and " Saba " (revelations of an old man). Supplementary works of a later date are the " Tikkunim " or " Tikkune ha-Zohar " (lit. " Supplements," " Supplements of the Zohar "), con- sisting of seventy chapters devoted entirely to a commentary on the word "Bereshith", and the "Zohar Chadash" ("the new Zohar"), which deals also with sections of the Song of Songs and the Book of Ruth.

The peculiar place occupied by the Zohar in the development of the Cabbalah is reflected in its language. Most of the Cabbalistic-mystic literature (as of older Jewish literature in general) is written in one or other of two languages—Hebrew and Aramaic. Of these Hebrew, broadly speaking, predominates in works of a didactic character, Aramaic in those of a more imaginative type. The language of the Zohar is for the most part an Aramaic to some extent akin to that of the early biblical translations and of many Midrashim. But the dialect of the Zohar is peculiar and seems to have sprung into being with the Zohar itself ; its Aramaic is full of Hebraisms and strange foreign words, and it employs a style and terminology of its own which give it a rich power of mystical expression on the basis of a somewhat scanty vocabulary. Within this basic style we can distinguish between the more modern and the more archaic, the more Aramaic and the more Hebraic, the more prosaic and the more poetical or rhetorical portions.[15] The numerous strange and artificial word-formations no doubt account for the presence in our texts of many enigmatic and corrupt passages.

Alike in diction and in composition the Zohar shows an extreme lack of finish, which greatly adds to its difficulty. It is full of inaccuracies, gaps, and repetitions in small things and great. The biblical verses which are subjected to mystical interpretation are not always taken in their original order. In virtue partly of the very nature of the cabbalistic tradition, certain biblical passages are given special prominence, while on the other hand whole sections of the Torah are omitted. The distribution is so uneven that the space devoted to the three last books of the Torah together barely equals that devoted to the first or second singly. It naturally accords with the scheme of the work that the Pentateuch and certain other biblical works, namely, Ezekiel, Daniel, Psalms, Ecclesiastes, and the

Song of Songs, should be treated differently from the rest of the Scriptures. The former, especially the books of the Torah, furnish—at least outwardly—the main themes, while the rest are cited only as they throw light on the subject in hand. The form of presentation is, like that of the Talmud, discursive, the mystical doctrine being interwoven with homiletical lessons, which are always attached to a Scriptural text. Discussions in the Zohar differ from those in the Talmud regarding the Halachah in the fact that mere sharpening of the intellect plays in them only a very subordinate role. Opinions which differ in themselves are yet linked together by a certain inner understanding between those who advance them, for the common objective of the esoteric investigation is to be attained not by the clash of argument, but by harmonious cooperation.

We have already touched on the question how far the talmudic scholars mentioned in the Zohar can be considered historically to have been mystics. With regard to the central figure of the Zohar, Simeon b. Yochai, there are a number of passages in the Talmud and Midrash[16] which on the one hand testify to his overweening mystical self-consciousness, and on the other hand pay high tribute to the holiness of his life. Thus we read : " Because of my merit, I am able to save from the Day of Judgment the world that has existed from the day of my birth to the day of my death." (Sukkah 45[2]). And in Midrash Shemoth Rabba (cap. 52) it is stated: "All Israel are under obligation to interrupt the study of the Torah in order to recite the Shema and the Eighteen Benedictions, except Simeon b. Yochai, because his whole life is devoted exclusively to heavenly subjects." Elsewhere (Bereshith Rabba, cap. 35) we find mention of an " epoch of Simeon b. Yochai ".

In the Zohar Simeon b. Yochai appears as the principal teacher and master, with seven disciples, who are occasionally designated his " seven eyes ". The legends about him[17], together with the main doctrines enunciated by him, form the kernel of the Zohar, which links organically

matters of everyday life with the heavenly spheres. As in
the Platonic dialogues, some everyday occurrence is often
commented on and made the starting-point for a discourse
or discussion on an abstruse subject. We are shown a
pair of Talmudists, perhaps Rabbi Chiya and Rabbi Isaac,
wandering from one town to another, and being joined
by the Shechinah when they discuss particularly deep
subjects, or meeting accidentally in an inn. At other
times the scholarly disciples appear in the Academy or
assemble round their master. We are also told much of
their inner life, their troubles, questions, and doubts. Sometimes we see them giving advice or help to fellow-men
whom they meet accidentally. Often too it happens that
such wandering scholars are joined by some stranger, it
may be a pack-carrier or ass-driver, or even a child, and
the celebrated authorities do not hesitate to receive the
teachings of wisdom from the simplest mouths. In these
brief and vivid touches we often seem to catch a breath
of the atmosphere of the Palestine of those days ; we have
the impression of direct contact, which may go back
to actual experience. Certainly those rabbinic scholars
who so often serve as the type of the argumentative,
" highbrow ", fanatical Pharisee, here show themselves
to us under quite another aspect—as inspired at all
times and seasons with inner love of wisdom, devoted
with childlike simplicity to the pursuit of divine love
and holiness.

Imperceptibly the whole atmosphere is changed first of
all perhaps only by trifling symbolical experiences or
occurrences, then more noticeably by the appearance of
the at first unrecognised " Holy Ancient " (a celestial being)
or the prophet Elijah as the master of the heavenly secrets.
The atmosphere of wonder plays above all round the figure
of Simeon b. Yochai, the " holy lamp " (*Buzina kadisha*).
who has been endowed with superhuman power over
heights and depths, and who is in this sense compared to
a tree " which reaches into both worlds ". While on some
occasions in the course of the narrative he expresses his

views simply as one of the company, on other occasions he is presented as the very pattern of the complete mystic, whose earthly pilgrimage itself is designated a period of mystical revelation, and whose discourses are listened to even by heavenly beings. His followers sometimes speak of him after his death with fond recollection, whilst in the Idra he still forms the bright centre of a circle of disciples, to whom before dying he transmits his holy heritage.

The halo which in the Zohar plays around the paths of mysticism as such is reflected in the names with which the mystics are designated, e.g., "Masters of the Teaching" (*Mare Mathnitin*), "Those who know the Measures" (*Yod'e Middin*), "Sons of Faith" (*Bene Mehemnutha*), "Reapers of the Field" (*Mechazde de-Chakla*), "Those worthy of Truth" (*Zakkae Keshot*), or "Wise of Heart" (*Chakime Liba*). They are however also called simply "maskilim" (intelligent—from Daniel, XII, 3, *v.* p. 85), a term which strangely enough has come into use in recent times for the diametrically opposite type—the "enlightened" who represent the modern "haskalah".

No sooner had the Zohar appeared than it was mentioned and made use of by contemporary Jewish writers—by Solomon ibn Adret who deals critically with the origin of the book, by Todros Abulafia, who cites it in his "Ozar ha-Kabod" (Treasury of Divine Glory), and by Menahem Recanati, who makes copious use of the Zohar in his mystical commentary on the Pentateuch.[18]

In the older sources the Zohar is called the Midrash of Rabbi Simeon b. Yochai (by Bachya ben Asher and Meir ibn Gabbai), also Midrash Yehi Or ("Let there be Light", by Zacuto), or "the Great Book, the Zohar" (by Recanati).

The Zohar was printed for the first time in 1558 at Cremona, and almost at the same time at Mantua. Among the numerous later editions those of Lublin, Amsterdam, Constantinople, and in later times Wilna, are the best known. A pointed edition originally published in Constantinople was issued afresh in miniature about twenty years ago by the Yalkut-Verlag in Berlin.

It goes without saying that a voluminous exegetical literature has grown up round the Zohar. Among the most important commentaries—most of which deal in detail only with selected portions of the work—are, next to a commentary on the Idroth assigned to Isaac Luria, those of Abraham Azulai (זהרי חמה), of Shalom Busaglo (מקדש מלך, הדרת מלך), of Baer ben Petachya (פתחי יה), and of the Gaon Elijah of Wilna, also some Chassidic commentaries, such as those by the Koznitzer Maggid (v. p. 144) and Dov Ber, the son of Schneur Zalman of Ladi.[19] There are also several indexes to the Zohar under the title of " Keys to the Zohar ".

There are not many translations. Earliest are the Latin translations of certain parts by Christian authors : of the Idroth in Knorr von Rosenroth's " Kabbala Denudata " (recently translated into English by Matters), and of the messianic portions in connection with Christian missions (e.g., by A. Tholuck in German). In English there exists a new fairly complete translation by H. Sperling and M. Simon. The Zohar was translated into French—very inaccurately—by Jean de Pauly, in a limited edition with numbered copies ; the Idra Zuta also earlier by Eliphaz Levi. Only small sections had been translated into German until a larger selection was issued in 1931 by the present writer, and since then Sholem has published the section dealing with the creation in a German translation. Finally mention may be made of a popular version in Yiddish from the 17th century, entitled " Nachlath Zewi ", by Zewi Hirsch Chotsch. Hebrew renderings of certain difficult expressions, ascribed to Chayim Vital, are printed in the margins of most Zohar editions under the title of " Derech Emeth " (Way of Truth). Later Hebrew translations, such as one by Hillel Zeitlin, have not appeared in print,[20] with the exception of that of Judah Rosenberg, in which the Zohar passages, often unfortunately torn from their contexts, are arranged according to the order of the texts in the Scripture.

Although in form the Zohar is the negation of system, it is imperative for the sake of the modern reader to make some attempt to present its doctrine in systematic shape.[21]

To begin with, the foundations and origin of the world are described in statements of fact or in symbolical pictures which form a cosmology in the widest sense of the term. Thus we are told of a primordial spark as a spaceless point out of which the Deity caused space to spring forth as a first envelopment (I, 152–16a). The same process is also denominated a primordial upwelling which is followed by a " radiation " and a " streaming forth ", two terms which in the Aramaic have closely allied meanings. As in the teaching of the Gnosis, the substance of the world is represented as being formed of light, specifically the " Or Kadmaa ", the hidden primordial light of the first day of the creation, which according to the Midrash is reserved for " the pious of the Future World ", in contrast with the visible light which was created on the fourth day, and which also out of its abundance gives forth another light which is not luminous (I, 156b). This is darkness, the dim primordial fire, the substance both of colours and of all material being. Another favourite figure for describing the process by which the world came into being is that of sowing or fructifying.

The central role in the work of creation is played by the " Word ". Here the Zohar comes into contact with the Alexandrian biblical exegesis. The close connection of the Word with light is indicated, according to the Zohar (II, 136b–137b), in the second verse of the 19th Psalm, which similarly links knowledge with darkness. In the account of the creation in Genesis also the Word first makes its appearance with the creation of light.

To explain the creative act of the Godhead the Zohar is satisfied with neither the popular conception of the Deity nor the popular story of the creation. An ultimate Being, the nature of which cannot even be inquired into, and which is therefore denominated simply " Who ",

creates for itself a " Palace " (Hechal), on which the Name
of God is stamped (I, 1*b*).

The immediate Creator of the world is not the divine
primordial Being. For creation there was required a second
principle which is identified with Metatron or the Messiah.
Thus we read in I, 33*b* : " R. Hiya said : God maketh the
earth by His strength (Jer. X, 12) .'He who made the
earth ' is the Holy One, blessed be He, above; 'by His
strength ' means ' by the Zaddik.' "[22]

The existing world is not the first ; it was preceded by
other worlds, which are symbolised by the Kings of Edom
mentioned in the thirty-sixth chapter of Genesis. The
creation of the world can therefore also be represented as
a process of purification and separation from " *tohu-wa-
bohu* ", the debris left over from preceding worlds. This
world of ours was, however, the first which, as taught also
in the Sefer Yezirah, was formed out of sounds and letters
belonging to the Name of God. So we read (I, 30*b*) : " And
the earth was void and without form. This describes the
original state . . . in which there was no substance, until
the world was graven with forty-two letters, all of which
are the ornamentation of the Holy Name. When they are
joined, letters ascend and descend, and form crowns for
themselves in all four quarters of the world, so that the
world is established through them and they through it.
A mould was formed for them like the seal of a ring ; when
they went in and issued, the world was created, and when
they were joined together in the seal the world was established. . . ." For this finally attained "establishment " of
the world, which is closely bound up with the existence of
man, the figure of the balance, i.e., of equilibrium, is often
used, as in the Sefer Yezirah. Thus at the opening of the
Sifra di Zeniuta we find : " A book weighed in the scales.
For before there was equilibrium, face could not look upon
face " (II, 176*b*).

Both the emanation doctrine of the Massechet Aziluth,
with its four stages of the development of the world, and
the doctrine of the Sefiroth are embodied in the Zohar,

where they are greatly amplified. Both the divine and the human being present a different aspect in the conditions of Aziluth and Beriah from that presented in the conditions of Yezirah and 'Asiyah, which are of a more physical character.

In relation to the Sefiroth the basis of being is designated as *En Sof* (" Without End ") or simply as *Ayin* (" Nothing "),[23] the dark undifferentiated background for an existence already differentiated though still immaterial.

The ten Sefiroth are arranged in three groups of three, later known as " the Intellect-world " (*Olam ha-muskal*), " the Soul or Feeling-World " (*Olam ha-murgash*), and " the Nature-world " (*Olam ha-mutba*), with the tenth Sefirah Malchuth the " Kingdom ", which combines in itself the contents of the higher being, i.e., the qualities of all the Sefiroth, in order to transmit them to man. The Sefiroth of the first triad are *Kether* (" Crown "), *Chokhmah* (" Wisdom "), and *Binah* (" Discernment ") ; of the second triad *Chesed* (" Grace "), *Pachad* (" Fear "), and *Tifereth* (" Beauty ") ; of the third triad *Nezach* (" Victory "), *Hod* (" Majesty "), and *Yesod* (" Foundation "). Besides this vertical division the Zohar uses also a horizontal one into a right, left, and centre section or " pillar " (*Amuda di-yamina, di-semola, di-meziuta*). To the first belong Chokhmah, Chesed, Nezach ; to the second Binah, Pachad, Hod ; to the central one Keter, Tifereth, Yesod, Malchuth.

Other designations and groupings are also found. Occasionally the En-Sof is fused with Keter, which then dominates the other Sefiroth. Again, between productive Wisdom (Chokhmah) and discriminating Reason (Binah) there is sometimes inserted a third element, Da'ath, or Knowledge.[24] The fourth Sefirah is called also *Gedulah* (" Greatness "), to express the universal love which pours itself forth unendingly, and the fifth *Geburah* (" Strength "), to express self-concentrating and limiting power. The two middle Sefiroth, of the right and left sides, *Chesed* and *Geburah*, correspond closely to the talmudical divine attributes of " Mercy " and " Severity ",[25] and after them the whole of the Right Side is designated " Pillar of Love " and the whole of the Left Side " Pillar of Judgment and Severity ". The sixth Sefirah, *Tifereth*, is called in virtue of its central position *Leb ha-Shamaim* (" Heart of the Heavens "). The ninth Sefirah *Yesod*, the " Foundation " of life, which combines the male and female creative powers, is often, as being the seat of the *Zaddik* (" Righteous One "), i.e., the Messiah, denoted *Zedek* (" Righteousness "), and the tenth Sefirah as being the seat of the Shechinah is itself called Shechinah, while a whole number of basic religious concepts (" Sabbath," " Peace," " Community of Israel ") are used also as descriptive appellations of the " Kingdom ".

In order to emphasise the organic connection of the Sefiroth, their totality is often pictured as a " tree ", or presented in the form of a man, each one corresponding to a different part of his organism (III, 296*a*).

As in the system of Joseph ibn Gikatilla, which however was perhaps derived from the Zohar, there are ten names of God corresponding to the ten Sefiroth.[26] Specially important in this connection is the assigning of the name YHWH to the principle of Love, and of the name Elohim to the principle of Judgment and Severity. The fact that these names after all designate only different sides of the divine essence seems to have obviated the danger of the individual Sefiroth being regarded as independent divine beings.

There is, however, also another way in which the rigid monotheistic conception seems to be infringed, namely, through a trinitarian element, which cannot be explained away, in the Godhead itself. There is mysterious mention in the Idra of " three heads of the Holy Ancient ", which in truth are after all only one (III, 288*a*). In the system of the Sefiroth also Chokhmah and Binah are opposed to one another as " Father " and " Mother ", or more precisely as " Upper Father " and " Upper Mother ". Similarly in Kether or Chokhmah the " Long-faced " (*Arich Anpin*)[27] is presented to us as " Father ", and in Tifereth the "Short-faced" (*Ze'er Anpin*) as "Son", while the maternal principle, under the title of "Lower Mother" or "Matron" (in Aramaic *Matronita*), appears in another guise in the Shechinah, that is, entwined within the tenth Sefirah. That a distinction is also made between "Son" and "Daughter" further complicates these very puzzling relations.[28]

The Sefiroth doctrine is brought into relation with actual life and conduct through its combination with a principle which the Zohar shares with ancient Egyptian teaching and which is formulated almost in the same words in the "Smaragdinic Tables", one of the "hermetic" writings which have come down to us from the later days of the ancient world. It runs : "What is above is also below, and what is below is also above." The implication is that the lower world mirrors the upper world, and that there is direct contact between them. The relation is one of reciprocal action, and the idea becomes an integral part of the Jewish religion in the belief that man below can influence the higher spheres, nay, that the stream of benediction from above must first be set in motion from below, or, in the language of the Zohar, that the "lower waters", which form the female element, must first approach the "upper waters", as the male element.

A note peculiar to the mysticism of the Zohar is to be found in the symbol of the union of the sexes, based upon certain expressions in the Song of Songs. As the separation of the "King", i.e. Tifereth, from the "Queen", i.e. the Shechinah, brings suffering and discord, so their union brings rapture and harmony to all worlds.

The angelology of the Zohar is derived from the older mysticism, and has its centre in the Merkabah (Aramaic, "*Reticha*"), in which beings of various grades and ranks appear united in a common task. The four "Beasts" give the key to four basic types of human nature, and are dominated by the four archangels (I, 71*b*, 211*a*). They are the real bearers and distributors of the higher life, which has its centre in the "storehouse of life".

Demons also appear in the Zohar. Their presence can be explained only by reference to the teaching of the Zohar on ethics in general. For the Zohar's idea of the universe it is essential that all ethical potentialities should have their origin in the macrocosmic organism, above all in the middle triad of the Sefiroth tree, and not merely in man.

The principle of evil has in the last resort to be located in the Left side, which is essentially the principle of negation. The Left side does not of itself represent evil, but its function is to supplement the absolute positive principle of the Right side by presenting an antithesis to it, a middle principle being further added to reconcile the two. This left, negative principle does not become evil before it puts itself in the place of the right, positive side. Then only does the left become the " other side ", a designation under which the Zohar, in its profound awe of a secret from which the veil is not to be readily lifted, comprehends everything inimical to existence. There is thus both a harmonious and a hostile opposition between the sides. To illustrate the harmonious opposition the Zohar compares it to the parting of the waters on the second day of the creation, in the account of which the possibility of evil is hinted in the omission of the formula " And God saw that it was good " ; while the hostile opposition is illustrated by the revolt of Korah (I, 17a).

In the doctrine of emanations, the contrast between positive and negative, which lies at the basis of that between good and evil, can be represented in its extreme form by the contrast between a region completely filled with existence or spirituality, and one on the outer confines of existence and devoid of spirit. In the series of emanations each one can always be regarded as the " envelope " or "house " of the one before it, a relation to which the figure of a nut with its shells is applied (I, 19b–20a). The periphery, however, forms no longer " houses ", but only " shells " (kelifoth), the last husks of existence which provide homes for the demonic beings, which roam ceaselessly through the world seeking to do harm (I, 55a, 204a).[29]

In the centre of existence, according to the Zoharic idea of the universe, stands man. This idea is expressed by the statement that the world acquired permanence only through the creation of man, that only with his appearance—as indicated in the second chapter of Genesis—did all other creatures become visible, and that the name of God was made complete only along with the human name of Abraham (I, 97b).[30]

The name " man " includes a number of meanings, distinct and yet connected : the divine prototype or primordial man, " Adam Kadmon " (in Aramaic *Adam Kadmaah*), the first man (*Adam ha-Rischon*)—both of these in a way including in themselves the whole of humanity —and the individual perishable man (usually termed *Bar Nash*, i.e. son of woman). Corresponding to the perfect primordial man there is further the future consummation of man in the person of the Messiah.

Man in general, whether cosmic or earthly, whether as race or as individual, has his real home in those exalted spheres in which the heavenly beings are also located. The Sefiroth tree which represents the world organism represents also the original spiritual form of man. Thus in ancient drawings we find various parts of the human organism assigned to various Sefiroth-regions—the brow to " Chokhmah ", the left temple to " Binah ", the two arms and the breast to the middle triad, all dominated by the " Crown " which hovers over the whole organism, while at the other end through the principle of " Kingdom " the spiritual man is shown connected with the ground through the feet. Thus, as the Zohar puts it, " the human form comprehends everything in itself, all that is in heaven and on the earth, the higher and lower beings ". And in the Tikkunim (Section I) we find the bold statement : " The form of man—that is the holy Shechinah."[31]

These facts may enable us to understand how it is that the Idroth, using a symbolism which is closely akin to that of the old Shiur Komah, and which is so hard for us to comprehend, can describe the divine essence itself with the organs and proportions of the human form. This becomes a little more intelligible to us when we remember that everything in the nature of our own looks and gestures is conceived of as being a direct expression of the spirit ; in fact, the Zohar, which contains also physiognomical observations, occasionally designates the body the " stamp " of the soul. It is worthy of note that the Zohar in its at once cosmic and religious conception of the human organism comes close to the talmudic tradition—also found already in the Targum Jonathan—according to which the number of bones in the human body, viz. 365, corresponds to that of the days of the year, while the number of its organs, viz. 248, corresponds to that of the prohibitions in the Torah. In this way, as in every mystical conception of the world, man is made to appear as the copy of the Cosmos—as " Mikrokosmos " (small universe), corresponding to the " Makrokosmos " (great universe) or " Makroanthropos " (greater man).

This correspondence holds good not only for man, but for the whole world of man, which as " earth " is opposed to the heavens. The same duality, however, applies also to the earth itself, a distinction being made between a " higher " celestial earth symbolically designated the " holy land ", and the " lower earth ", the world of our daily life. In that upper earth dwelt also the first man before he descended to our earth, in the " Garden of Eden ". As in the scriptural text itself, a distinction is made between the " garden " and " Eden ". By the system of letter-mysticism, " Gan " (garden) is made to indicate the source of body and soul (" Guf " and " Neshamah "), while " Eden " designates the totality of the heavenly powers which stream into it, and from which in turn spring the streams which fructify the earthly life. This focus of life is also, in accordance with the traditional interpretation of 1 Sam., XXV, 29, denominated the " gathering of life " (Zeror ha-Chayim).

In the original condition of man before his sin the " garment ", i.e., the body, is still of the nature of light, the image of God is still visible in it, and the whole of Nature looks up with reverence to man who is still linked with his heavenly origin and endowed with all wisdom. Only in consequence of sin does the divine image forsake him, his body becomes darkened, and inferior beings like the beasts are able to inspire in. him the sense of fear (I, 71a).

Yet though the body of man mirrors heavenly mysteries, his real essence is constituted by his soul. As in almost all theosophic and many philosophic systems,[32] the soul in the Zohar is represented as threefold. The three designations found in the Scripture—*Nefesh*, *Ruach*, and *Neshamah* —are taken to indicate three grades of the soul in its relation to the upper and the lower world. Nefesh (lit. " vitality ") provides man with his feelings and impulses, with everything which externally connects him with the earthly world and which internally he has in common with the beasts. At the other end of the scale is Neshamah (lit. " breathing "), which is the " breath " of higher spirituality, the bridge which connects him with the heavenly world. The connecting link between the two is constituted by the Ruach (lit. " air "), the proper organ of the inner life of the soul, its own inner breath (the *neshamah* being half external), which forms but an isolated fragment of the universal spiritual life, from which it also derives its name. Yet strictly speaking these three kinds of soul[33] are not separate parts of the human soul, which is essentially one, and their activities are intermingled. Thus the human being in this also reproduces its divine prototype, in which three powers form a single essence (I, 205b–206c, 83b). This unity of the soul is, as in the Provençal Jewish mysticism, designated with the simple name " I " (*ani*). Certainly with this name the Zohar denotes not so much the individual unity as that cosmic-divine unity from which the individual unity springs, and which in the more emphatic form *Anochi* stands so conspicuously at the head of the Decalogue. Hence this " I " is occasionally identified with the Shechinah (I, 85a).

The higher, most spiritual part of the soul is also, as in Gabirol, designated the "speaking" part, i.e., the soul which has command of words, since in virtue of this capacity it most profoundly mirrors the divine nature (III, 48a, 46b–47a). The spoken word itself, like the soul, has three grades—breathing, voice, and word properly so called (i.e., the meaning of the word).[34]. On its material side it is formed from the three higher elements, Fire, Air, and Water. This is indicated by the analysis of the root A-M-R- (word, to speak) into A-ish (fire), M-ayim (water), and R-uach (air). Thus the continuation of the Logos in human speech forms one of the most intimate connections of man with the divine origin. The Zohar occasionally expresses this idea by identifying the Temple of God with the human organ of speech.

The relation of the soul to the body is naturally a subject to which the Zohar pays particular attention. The first entry of the soul into the body at birth is a perpetual wonder, to which the Zohar sometimes applies the verse of the Psalms, "How great are Thy works, O Lord". Just as death is an ascent to the heavenly spheres, so birth is only a descent of the soul from the "upper" to the "lower" Garden of Eden, and thence to the earth itself. Already at the moment of conception the child in ethereal form hovers over the parental couple (I, 233b). And previous to birth the soul has a meeting with the divine primordial man at the threshold of both worlds (I, 57b). Then accompanied by the good and the evil impulse man lives through his allotted days, which are preserved for him in actual existence up to the hour of his death and judgment (I, 22b). The conduct of man in the moral sphere testifies to the kind of supra-sensual powers with which he has been connected ; with his good deeds he attracts to himself beneficent beings, and with his evil deeds demonic. After his death his abode in the Beyond is determined by his manner of life on earth.

Man is exposed continuously to cosmic influences which issue from the stars, or more precisely from the spiritual beings which work through the stars (I, 276), an idea which is also found in Aristotle. Further, the planets stand in mysterious connection with the organs of the human body, Saturn with the spleen, Jupiter with the liver, and Mars with the gall. From the excess of these three influences spring the three sins which the Talmud regards as cardinal—adultery, idolatry, and murder.

In sleep the soul is dominated by the Nefesh, just as by day the Ruach is dominant. The highest part of the soul then ascends to heavenly regions, in order to behold the presence of the King. Dreams, which according to the Talmud form a sixtieth part of prophecy, are one of the means through which everything which is to happen is announced beforehand.[35]

Sleep is also a fleeting image of the process of death, in which the three parts of the soul separate from one another. Nefesh for a time hovers over the body, thus causing the "pangs of the grave". Ruach enters the lower, Neshamah the upper Garden of Eden (III, 141b–142a). For a time the deceased retains the form of his body, but later he is endowed with a new and finer body for his life in the higher realms of existence (III, 70a, I, 65b). At the gateway of his higher existence man again meets the Adam Kadmon, his heavenly prototype.

The legends related of Simeon b. Yochai and his disciples show that for the souls of the initiated the manner of ascent into the higher realms of existence is somewhat different, in virtue of their having been more or less in direct contact with these regions even in their earthly life, so that the heavenly beings already listen to the Master while teaching here on earth, and the manner in which the teaching is carried on in the Academy has its counterpart in the "Upper Academy" (Hebr. *Yeshibah shel Ma'alah*, Aramaic, *Metibta 'Ilaah*).

The Zohar teaches also, like the Pythagoreans, the ancient Indians, and the modern occultists, a doctrine of transmigration of souls. This is called *Gilgul*, i.e., circuit (III, 215b–216a). The union of a married couple is for instance only the rediscovery of one another by two souls which were united before birth (I, 49b–50a). This belief is one sign of the importance attached by the Zohar to the earthly life, in spite of its predominating concern with the supra-terrestrial. From the same outlook springs the high importance attached to the physical begetting of man and everything connected with it. This is illustrated by the belief that if a man has not contributed to the physical work of creation by the begetting of offspring, certain higher spheres of existence remain closed to him after death.

It is to be noted that purely ethical precepts are rarely found in the Zohar. The right way for a man consists only in his finding his proper connection with the " upper " and " lower " worlds. " A man by his actions is always drawing to himself some emissary from the other world, good or evil according to the paths which he treads " (I, 53b). The felicity also which is obtained by fulfilment of the divine precept consists in nothing else than in being brought into touch with the beneficence which streams from the higher worlds.

The conduct of a man can lead him to the desired goal in two ways—through ascent and through return (teshubah). Of these ways the latter is superior, and its spiritual possi-bilities are boundless. For it springs from an impulse which is part of the general impulse of the world trying to return to God. After death the penitent attains to higher stages of existence than the perfectly righteous. The goal itself is a more universally human or an almost superhuman one. The Zohar is never weary of praising the lot of those who have discovered how to link themselves with the celestial worlds. And an infinitely more exalted task awaits the elect who have attained this—themselves to co-operate in the work of God.

In the same way two types are to be distinguished in the central act of the religious life, in prayer. There is the prayer of the " poor " and the prayer of the " righteous ", the former more pure in its impulse, the latter more elevated

in itself. The former is offered by the man who is completely absorbed in God, who has nothing of his own, who
keeps his whole being open like a cistern in order to fill
it with the stream of benediction from heaven, with the
divine love. The other is offered by the man who has
himself already become a source of well-being, who himself
in ever-growing measure effects the connection with the
streams of heavenly blessing.

Certainly suffering is an essential ingredient in the life
of the righteous. Seen in its proper light, it is just this
that testifies the deeper love of God for him. Thus we
read (I, 180b) : " The world is thus governed in mercy,
and thereby is able to endure. But, you may ask, is not
a man often punished by God, and undeservedly ? The
answer is . . . that when suffering befalls a righteous
man, it is on account of the love which God bears to him.
He crushes his body in order to give more power to his
soul, so that He may draw him nearer in love. For it is
needful that the body should be weak and the soul strong,
so that a man may be beloved of God . . . that the Holy
One inflicts suffering on the righteous in this world in order
that they may merit the world to come. But he who is
weak of soul and strong of body is hated of God." . . .

Man's spirit soars to its greatest heights in the whole-
hearted search for truth. In an elucidation of the Ten
Commandments, the Zohar speaks of a neglect " to put
things in their right places "—an expression to which
something similar is already found in the Sefer Yezirah.[36]
The idea is that a proper conception of reality on the part
of man repeats in a way the original act of creation—shows
things their right place in the concatenation of worlds.
And confusion in this conception produces to some extent
confusion in the scheme of things itself. This relation of
man—especially of the religious man—to truth is indicated
by the Hebrew language itself which makes *emeth*, truth,
the root of *emunah*, faith. The favourite term of the Zohar
for expressing the connection of the *illuminati* with the
upper worlds is *Bene Mehemnuta*, " sons of faith " (*v.* p. 92),

or, as we might also translate in virtue of its etymology, " sons of truth ".

This highest stage at the same time confers on man his highest and most characteristic *power*. Such power is not to be acquired by occult methods of controlling natural forces, which are often used for selfish or harmful purposes, still less by the childish play of word and number magic. If we find in the Zohar such plays on words and juggling with letters and numbers, side by side with passages of striking profundity, this is to be assigned rather to mere naiveté than to any magical purpose. Also the element of the marvellous, of which the legends of the Master and his disciples are so full, is by no means inserted in the Zohar thoughtlessly or at random. It was, however, only in later times that Jewish mysticism developed the conception that continuous activity in communion with God was after all the real miracle performed by men. For behind it stands the permanent wonder of the connection and the correspondence of the lower and upper worlds.

The perfected activity of man has a threefold beneficial effect. In the first place, on the man himself, since in pouring forth blessing the spheres of existence which are nearest to him depend on what they themselves receive from man. Secondly, human activity becomes helpful for the fulfilment of the divine work itself. This is indicated by the double meaning of the word " blessing " in the language of the Bible, applying as it does both to God and to man.[37] Lastly the activity of man, as continuation of the work of God and as his contribution to it, penetrates into the regions beneath him which through his struggles and victories become subject to him or are forced to assist him. Thus in this blessing above and below is fulfilled the true ascent, the real magical performance of man. The Zohar sometimes expresses this stage of perfection by calling the pious man " the fruit of God's work " (I, 82b).

The views on man which we have here set forth do not form, to outward appearance, the chief subject of the Zohar.

This is to be found rather in the interpretation of the biblical history, an interpretation which goes beyond the boundaries of the original on both sides—backwards into the pre-terrestrial and supra-terrestrial spheres of creation, and forwards into a Messianic future.

Mystical interpretation is applied particularly to those oldest parts of the biblical history in which symbolism and reality, or, more precisely, celestial and terrestrial events are almost inextricably interwoven.[38] And while the Zohar usually commences by accepting the biblical account literally and in all simplicity, it often ends by giving it a symbolical turn, reminding us of Philo.

While, for the Zohar, the creation of the world reaches its termination with the formation of Adam, the historical process commences to a certain extent with the transgression of the first human pair, since it is this which produces confusion in the upper and lower worlds and after it mankind goes through ever new phases of guilt and repentance. From this point of view historical events assume the character of a religious process. The guarantee for the continued existence of the world lies in the repeatedly renewed " Covenant ", the three first main stages of which are realised through Noah (in the rainbow), through Abraham (in the circumcision), and through Moses (in the Sinaitic covenant).

The three Patriarchs represent on the one side stages of the revelation of the Godhead, on the other side the distinguishing qualities assigned by the Cabbalah to certain of the Sefiroth. Abraham represents the quality of loving grace, Isaac of stern justice, and Jacob-Israel of perfect righteousness. The triad is raised to the tetrad of the Merkabah by the inclusion of Joseph, or, in another interpretation, of David, who is supposed to have united himself with the Patriarchs during his seven years' reign in Hebron, the city of their graves.

Messianic traits are attributed especially to Joseph, who is a replica of his father on a higher plane. Of him we are told (I, 180a) : " When Jacob was brought to rest in Joseph and so the sun was united with the moon, then there commenced a production of offspring, the progenitor being Joseph. For it is that perennially flowing stream which fructifies the earth and from which generations are propagated in the world. For the sun, even when he approaches the moon, cannot cause vegetation without the help of that grade which goes under the name of Righteous (*Zaddik*). It was then Joseph who was the grade of Jacob to bear fruit and bring forth offspring into the world."

The symbolic character of the biblical exegesis of the Zohar comes out in the idea that besides the " lower " patriarchs there are also " upper " ones, in the mention of an " upper High Priest ", an " upper King David ", etc. Many biblical figures are given partly or wholly a symbolic significance, e.g., Canaan, Lot, Esau, Rachel, Bath-sheba. Countries and places are also assigned a definite symbolic sense, e.g., Egypt is the home of (spiritual) darkness. The wilderness is placed in a new light through the etymological connection of its Hebrew name " Midbar " with " Dabar ", the " word " which comes to life in it.

This symbolical style of interpretation raises an important question with regard to the Zohar's conception of the " Covenant ". Is this covenant confined to Israel, or is the name " Israel " itself used symbolically for the whole of humanity ? The application of this name to cosmic potencies, as in the designation of the tenth Sefirah as " Community of Israel " (*Keneseth Israel*), speaks for this symbolic sense. On the other hand, however, the intense belief of the Zohar in the religious importance of the people of Israel makes it difficult to accept this idea. We should rather say that Israel is presented at once as reality and symbol, the assumption being that this people with its history of spiritual struggle, with its moral advances and lapses, with its despair and its hopes, with its alternations of separation from and approach to God, is meant to be a symbol, that is to say, a concrete type and central example for all humanity. Hence the covenant which has been made directly with Israel is also made indirectly through Israel with the whole of mankind. The Zohar, like the Talmud, expresses this by saying that the fate of Israel does not depend on any special " constellation " (*mazzal*), or any special " Prince " (*Sar*) but is directly subjected to the divine control.

Along with the people the Land of Israel is also of prime significance, both symbolical and actual. It forms the centre of the earth, and its material substance is like that of the first man, brought together from the whole of the earth. According to another conception, the holy land is the central point from which the whole earth has been planted. This central character is accentuated in Jerusalem and in the Sanctuary, which exists both above and below.[39] The name of Zion is in fact, like that of " Community of Israel " (*v. supra*), applied to the tenth Sefirah, that of the " Kingdom ". And the love of the " King " and the " Queen ", which is sung in the Song of Songs as the love of Solomon for the Shulammite, is nothing else than the love of God for Zion. The Hebrew language is also of primary importance. It is the one original language which gave unity, and with it strength, even to the rebels who built the Tower of Babel (I, 75b), and also the one language which is understood by the angels.

In the centre of the land stood the Temple, which with its service formed the focus of the religious life of ancient Israel. The Zohar gives also the symbolic sense of the materials, colours and dimensions of all parts and components of the Tent of Meeting and of the Temple. The deepest significance is attached to the sacrifice, which of course is no mere external ceremonial act, but which brings the inmost intention of the worshipper to the throne of the Almighty. Its efficacy in linking the human with the divine is expressed by the likeness of a flame consisting of three grades. One is dark and continuously consumes a material substance (e.g. the wick), by which it is maintained and nourished. This fire, however, continuously dissolves itself into a constant white light,[40] which consumes nothing, but rests in itself; and over this hovers yet another which is invisible.

The whole passage, slightly abbreviated, runs as follows : " We may say that he who desires to penetrate the mystery of the holy unity should contemplate the flame which rises from a burning coal or candle. The flame cannot rise save from some concrete body. . . . Further, in the flame itself there are two lights : one white and luminous, and the other black or blue. The white light is the higher of the two and rises steadily. . . . The lower light is . . . a connecting link between the white light to which it is attached above and the concrete body to which it is attached below, and which keeps it alight. This light always consumes anything which is under it or which is brought in contact with it, for such is its nature, to be a source of destruction and death. But the white light which is above it never consumes or destroys and never changes. Therefore Moses said, ' For the Lord thy God is a consuming fire '—literally consuming all that is beneath Him. That is why he said, ' *thy* God ' and not ' *our* God ', because Moses was in that white light above which does not consume or destroy. Now observe. The impulse through which this blue light is set aflame and attaches itself to the white light comes only from Israel who cleave to it from below. Further, although it is the nature of this blue or black light to consume everything that is in contact with it beneath, yet Israel are able to cleave to it from below and still exist ; so it is written, ' And ye that cleave to the Lord your God are all of you alive this day '. *Your* God and not *our* God : to wit, that blue or black flame which consumes and destroys all that cleaves to it from below ; yet you cleave and are still alive. Above the white light and surrounding it is still another secret light, symbolical of the supreme essence. Thus the ascending flame symbolises the highest mysteries of wisdom. . . ."

And again : " This is the secret of the sacrifice. The ascending smoke kindles the blue light, which then attaches itself to the white light, so that the whole candle is completely alight. Since it is the nature of the blue light to destroy and consume everything which is in contact with it underneath, when the sacrifice is pleasing and the candle is completely alight, then . . . in the case of Elijah the fire of the Lord descends and consumes the burnt-offering " (1 Kings, XVIII, 38), " this being a manifestation that the chain is complete, the blue light both cleaving to the white light and consuming the fat and the flesh of the burnt-offering beneath it, for it does not consume what is beneath it save when it ascends and attaches itself to the white light. Then there is peace in all worlds and the whole forms a unity " (I, 50*b*–51*b*).

The two principal names applied to the sacrifice indicate by their etymological significance the two methods of approach to God. They are *Olah*, or burnt-offering (literally " that which ascends "), and *Korban*, or offering (lit. " that which is brought near "). The sacrifice is a real connection with the upper worlds, and its acceptance is revealed in the mighty vision of Uriel, who becomes visible in the form of a lion crouching over his prey (III, 33*a*). A special function is assigned to the sacrifice which on the Day of Atonement is brought, in the form of one of the two he-goats, to Azazel, the representative of the principle of evil. It possesses a potency which diverts and mollifies the " Accuser ", and even turns him into an " Advocate "—that is to say, transforms evil itself into good.

The festivals derive their mystical significance from their relation to the Sefiroth, to the powers of Grace and Stern Judgment, to the positions of the sun and the moon. A special character is given to the month of Tishri by the fact that on the day of New Year, when the Accuser seeks to set in motion " stern justice ", the sound of the Shofar, uniting in itself the elements of fire, water, and air, ascends to the heavenly throne and rouses the power of Grace. Then, on the Day of Atonement, " the Holy One, blessed be He, is able to judge the world in love, since the power of love has now united itself with the power of justice " (I, 141*a*). And this union again is connected with the change from the obscuring of the moon on the New Year's day to the harmonious conjuncture of sun and moon on the Day of Atonement.

The covenant, however, finds its most visible expression in the institution of the Sabbath,[41] the character of which corresponds to that of the seventh day of the Creation, which belonged not to the actual work, but to a higher stage of it, the completion. The Sabbath elevates man above nature, Israel above the mass of the peoples. On Sabbath too the power of justice, and with it of evil, is shut out. This day stands completely under the standard of love. Its reconciling power is so great that it soothes even the suffering and torture of the evil spirits and of the souls of men performing expiation after death. On Sabbath and Festivals man is joined by a heavenly soul-companion, the *Neshamah Yeterah* ("extra soul"), since on those days there is a closer connection with the source of all souls than on other days. The three Sabbath meals, which were later to acquire such significance in the Lurian Cabbalah and in Chassidism, designate stages of the Sabbath delight and sanctification as realised in the earthly sphere.

It is particularly the original blessing of the Sabbath which, no longer confined to the epoch of the theocratic state, is able to accompany Israel into exile and dispersion. It therefore brings out into the strongest relief the soothing and comforting power of the Shechinah, so much so that "Sabbath" and "Shechinah" become interchangeable as designations of the tenth Sefirah. The symbolism of the Song of Songs, the love of God for the Community of Israel, is consummated in the intimacy and tender glow of the Sabbath love, so that the Shechinah receives from the Sabbath the appellation of "bride", endowed with the ever youthful bloom of a divine beauty. Hence the Sabbath is connected more closely than any other symbol with its supra-terrestrial prototype, the "lower" with the "upper" Sabbath.

Ceremonial precepts are occasionally treated symbolically in the Zohar, e.g. the plants used in the Feast of Tabernacles, and particularly the phylacteries, which contain the declaration of God's unity in the *Shema*, and which are assigned to the head and the heart, or also to the right and the left side. Ceremonial prayers are also dealt with in the same way, especially the *Shema*, the wording of which mirrors the divine unity in trinity, and the *Kedushah*, in explaining which the Zohar follows the Merkabah mysticism.

In dealing with the Torah, the central feature of the Jewish religious system, embracing not only the Pentateuch and the laws, but the whole teaching in its widest sense, the Zohar adopts the same view as the Talmud, that the Torah preceded the creation of the world, serving as its prototype. The Zohar also, like the Talmud, is never weary of extolling the lot of those who devote their life to its study. In the full sense of the term, however, the Torah is practised only by those who penetrate beneath its surface into its inner meaning. The old doctrine of the seventy methods of interpreting the Torah is reflected in such words as the following of R. Simeon (in the Idra Rabba) : " Unhappy is the man who sees in the interpretation of the Torah the recital of a simple narrative told in words of ordinary usage. Were it only that, we should have no difficulty in composing a better and more attractive Torah to-day. But the words we read are only the outer cloak. Each one of them contains a higher meaning than that which is apparent to us. Just as they who would judge a man only by his outer garments are bound to be disappointed, for it is the body and the spirit which make the man. Under the garments of the Torah, which are the words, and under the body of the Torah, which is the commandments, lies the soul, which is the hidden mystery (III, 152a, abridged after Benzion).

He who occupies himself with the Torah every day has a share in the future world. And when the elect investigate the mysteries of the Torah in the midnight hours, the Most Holy receives their souls in the Garden of Eden, where He disports Himself with them in an ecstasy of delight.[42] And when new discoveries are made in the course of studying the Torah, they are not only inscribed in a heavenly book, but they contribute to the production of " a new heaven and a new earth ".

Although the Zohar occasionally, if not very often, treats talmudical precepts also symbolically, a certain repugnance to talmudic ritualism is revealed in certain sarcastic observations, e.g., in the remark : " The grave of Moses is the Mishnah."

Epochs and personalities of the post-Mosaic period are only occasionally referred to in the Zohar. The character of certain epochs is in part determined by the conjuncture of the sun and the moon which dominates them. Thus, for instance, the moon obtains its full illumination from the sun in the time of King Solomon.

Through its sins, however, Israel has given the " other side " entry into the Holy Land. And the Exile places Israel completely under the dominion of a " strange power ", that is, of an alien celestial control. While, however, the immediate divine blessings are withheld from Israel in the period of exile, during which the sun has ceased to illumine the moon, the Shechinah follows it like a loving mother through dispersion and humiliation. Thus a " thread of grace " still plays round Israel in its abandoned and forsaken state, and suffering and misfortune cannot destroy its confidence that the tent of David, the " tent of peace ", will one day again be erected, and the ejected spouse will be restored to her rightful place. And it is mysteriously whispered that, if this time Israel will no longer be able to effect its return by means of its own strength, salvation will come to it from the very source, the husband will himself bring back his banished spouse (III, 6 a, b).

The coming of the Messiah at the end of days is only distantly hinted at. The cosmic significance of the Messiah plays a great part in the whole conception of the Zohar. He is the " foundation stone of the world "[43] and also the *Zaddik*, " the ever-living one ", who like a tree with its root in one domain and its branches in another is able to be in both worlds at once. In virtue of the text " the

Zaddik is the foundation of the world " (*Yesod Olam*), he also appears as a designation of the ninth Sefirah, *Yesod.*

The heavenly region from which the Messiah will come at the end of days is called " the Bird's Nest ", and the place of his appearance on earth is specified as Galilee.[44] Here and there traces are found of the talmudic conception of a twofold Messiah ; mention is also made of the terrible world-wide conflicts, with their threat to the very existence of Israel, which will precede the establishment of the ultimate Kingdom of Peace.[45] The work of salvation will be accomplished in three stages : the gathering of Israel, the erection of the Sanctuary—which, however, is sometimes conceived only symbolically—and the resurrection of the dead, through the dew which flows from the head of the " Long of Face ".[46] The idea of the redemption culminates in apocalyptic visions, partly taken from the prophets, according to which in those last struggles one star will swallow up seven others, and finally (as prophesied in Isaiah, XXX, 26), " the light of the moon will be equal to that of the sun ". And in those days, which will see the purification not only of individuals but of the world, the most profound mysteries will become nothing more than mere child's knowledge.

This period also, however, in which, with the concurrence of the higher world, higher secrets will be revealed, has its special significance for the process of initiation as described by the Zohar. The precise manner may be seen from the following account taken from the Idra Rabba (III, 128*a*) :

" He (R. Simeon) called R. Eleazar his son and commanded him to sit down before him and R. Abba on the other side, and said : ' We are the consummation of all. Thus far we are standing firmly.' They kept silence and they heard a voice and their knees knocked against one another with fear. What was the voice ? The voice of the Holy Assembly which was assembling above. R. Simeon rejoiced and said : ' O Lord, I have heard Thy voice and was afraid. O Lord, revive Thy work in the midst of the years, in the midst of the years make known ; in wrath remember mercy (Hab. III, 2).' And he continued : ' There fear was in place, but our condition is dependent upon love, as it is written : And thou shalt love the Lord thy God with all thy heart and with all thy soul and with all thy might (Deut. VI, 5) . . . and also : I have loved you, said the Lord (Mal. I, 2).' "

NOTES TO CHAPTER VI.

[1] A German translation of the Book Bahir, with copious notes, was published in 1923 by Gerhard Sholem.

[2] On the first page of the text of the Zohar proper, after the 14-page introduction and a brief digression on the creation doctrine. The quotation is followed by some short passages each beginning with the word "Zohar". A similar entitling of the book as "Zohar" is found in III, 153b, where also it is somewhat strangely called "the Book of Noah".

[3] On the author of the books Kana and Peliah as his reputed descendant, v. p. 82.

[4] Among the authorities mentioned in the Book Bahir are R. Amora, Berechiah, Bun, and Rechumai, besides well known Tannaitic scholars like R. Johanan, Meir, and Judah.

[5] This idea is mentioned also by Spinoza at the beginning of his Hebrew Grammar as "being derived from the Rabbis".

[6] V. p. 49.

[7] Translated by Sholem "Logoi".

[8] Of the life of Moses ben Shemtob of Leon little is known. He was born in Leon and lived in many places—Valladolid, Guadalajara, Avila, and finally Alviero, where according to the account of Abr. Zacuto (v. supra) he died in 1305. His book Sefer ha-Nefesh ha-chakhamah "Book of the Wise Soul"), also called "Sefer ha-Mishkal" (Book of Weighing), and first printed in 1608, contains a mystical doctrine of the soul, based on Ibn Gabirol's distinction of the vegetable, animal, and rational souls. Its main themes are the nature of the soul, its state after death, the "future world", and the resurrection.

[9] A similar account is given by Gedaliah ibn Yachya in "Shalsheleth ha-Kabbalah."

[10] Unfortunately the account breaks off just before coming to the information which Zacuto says he received from a disciple of Moses de Leon.

[11] The high antiquity of the Zohar is maintained by among others the Cabbalist and poet Moses Chayim Luzzatto (in the 18th century), David Luria (in his work Kadmuth Sefer ha-Zohar), and Mose Kunitz in his book on Simeon b. Yochai. Among the opponents of this view are the Renaissance period scholars Leo de Modena (in his Ari Nohem) and Elia del Medigo (in the work Mazref la-Hokhmah), and also Jacob Emden in his controversy with Jonathan Eibeschütz and in his work Mitpachath Soferim.

[12] In the article מפתח למפר הזהר in the 6th, 7th and 8th volumes of " Ha-Tekufah ".

[13] Reminding us of the frequent designation of Christ as " Pastor Fidelis ".

[14] The central figure in the Pirke di R. Eliezer, an ancient Midrash.

[15] Thus, e.g., the Tosefta in II, 42b, has a kind of verse-rhythm which was afterwards imitated by Isaac Luria in his poems.

[16] These have been collected by Mose Kunitz.

[17] These have been very attractively presented by Azriel Benzion in his work on the Zohar.

[18] It is also mentioned in the Fox Fables of Isaac ibn Sahula.

[19] V. p. 44 sqq..

[20] A small part has recently appeared in the " Mezudah " annual (London, 1943).

[21] For older or more detailed presentation the reader may be referred to the works of Ad. Franck, M. Joel, K. Stern, S. Karppe, and I. Myer (V. Index). A survey of the Zohar literature in general is given in the section dealing with the subject in Sholem's " Bibliographia Kabbalistica " ; see also the bibliographical data in the same author's " Major Trends of Jewish Mysticism ".

[22] For the Zaddik as a designation of the Messiah v. p. 115.

[23] The " Ayin " as ultimate principle of existence again appears as the " Nichtsein " standing behind the " Sein " in the German philosopher Hegel, and even earlier in Jacob Böhme (v. ch. IX).

[24] The trinity of Chokhmah, Binah, Daath, is based on scriptural verses (Ex. XXXI, 3 ; XXXV, 31), while Chokhmah and Binah (otherwise Tebunah) often appear in conjunction in the Bible.

[25] V. p. 167.

[26] See the Appendix in Vol. I of the Soncino Press translation of the Zohar.

[27] Ehrenpreis regards אריך אנפין simply as the Aramaic translation of the Hebrew ארך אפים, the " long-suffering ".

[28] In spite of its difference from the Christian dogma, the " trinity " in the Zohar was often adduced by Christian Cabbalists and missionary writers (cf. Ch. IX).

[29] Besides the primeval serpent on which Samael rides the Zohar is well acquainted with all the demonic beings which are mentioned in the Talmud and Midrash, among them also the " evil inclination ", and has also descriptive appellations for those beings which cause death, destruction, sickness, and sin. The activity of the Serpent is connected with the obscuration of the moon (I, 193a, b).

[30] Through the analysis of the name of God אלהים into אלה+מי, and of אברהם into אבר+מה.

[31] An illustration of this kind is to be found in the Jewish Encyclopedia and in the book of I. Myer. In a similar manner in astrological works twelve parts of the human organism were assigned to the twelve signs of the Zodiac.

[32] Cf. especially Gen. II, 7.

[33] The triple division of the human organism takes different forms in the Platonic and Aristotelian philosophy, in the medieval religious philosophy, and in modern anthroposophy, which, with its division into "sentient soul", "rational soul", and "conscious soul", comes fairly near to the Zohar.

[34] In many texts of the Sefer Yezirah we find the expression קול ורוח ודבור (I, 9).

[35] These revelations were made originally by prophets, then by the "Wise" (*Chakhamin*), later only through dreams and the flight of birds.

[36] The words are: "To settle the Fashioner (of the world) in his place " (IV, 2).

[37] On this see Hugo Bergmann's "Die Heiligung des Namens".

[38] A modern mystic (Rudolf Steiner) remarks that the often imperceptible transition from the natural to the super-natural forms one of the most marked traits of the biblical narrative.

[39] On the "Upper Sanctuary" *v.* the treatise of Aptowitzer on the subject.

[40] The "consuming fire" represents both sides of the principle of Stern Justice, which can act both beneficently and destructively.

[41] The name of Sabbath is brought into connection with that of Seth the son of Adam (שת, שית, שבת) who symbolises the firm establishment of the world.

[42] This idea is based especially on the nightly harp-playing of King David. From it was derived the later custom of "midnight prayer", which includes also readings from the Zohar.

[43] He is also therefore, as with Paul, the "corner stone" of Ps. CXVIII, 22.

[44] Whether there is some allusion to Christianity here cannot be determined. In any case this idea was cultivated in the mystical circle of Isaac Luria, which had its centre in Galilee.

[45] *V.* I, 119a *sqq.*

[46] According to the Zohar, at the resurrection of the dead the soul will again be united with the same body as in this life. Since, however, the soul has passed through many incarnations and through many bodies, we must understand by this body the last one which has already attained its permanence. In the Messiah's time too the stock of souls to be sent down to earth will have been exhausted. (See on this also L. Bendavid, "Ueber den Glauben der Juden an einen künftigen Messias"). With the idea of incarnation is also joined the fantastic notion that it is only the pious in the Holy Land who will rise again, and that therefore the bodies buried in other lands must first roll through subterranean cavities to the Holy Land.

VII

THE PERIOD OF THE LURIAN AND LATER CABBALAH

Concurrently with the recognition by Cabbalists of the Zohar as the central work of the Cabbalah, that doctrine itself became more and more closely intertwined with the whole religious life of Judaism. A new phase in its history began with the migration of the Jews from Spain and Portugal, after the expulsion, to the Orient, and especially to the Holy Land. Here the Zohar was studied with renewed zest, and in the sixteenth century, side by side with numerous prominent Talmudists, a circle of leading Cabbalists was formed in the holy city of Safed (Zefath). And without being strictly a student of the Cabbalah, the celebrated author of the Shulchan Aruch, Joseph Caro,[1] the *doyen* of the Safed community, could also be reckoned as a mystic on account of his work " Maggid Mesharim " (מגיד מישרים. He who shows the right Way, *v.* Isaiah, xlv, 19), which contains descriptions of visions received by him through an angel after whom the book is entitled, and who, as the personified Mishnah, guides the author in all critical occasions of his life and solves for him difficult religious questions.

The most notable of Caro's disciples were Moses ben Chayim Alsheikh[2] and Moses Cordoveiro.[3] The former was a celebrated preacher and wrote also a mystical commentary to the Bible. Moses Cordoveiro is the great encyclopædist of the older Cabbalah. His principal work, which later was also translated into Latin, was the " Pardes Rimmonim " (Garden of Pomegranates), containing a systematic exposition of the Cabbalistic doctrine as found in the Zohar.[4] He deals particularly with fundamental problems of the Creation, and, in connection with these, with the nature of the Sefiroth, which he conceives not so much as beings (" Azamoth ") but rather as vessels (" Kelim ") which render possible a manifold functioning of the single

Godhead. This relation between the Divine essence and the
Sefiroth was later frequently compared with that which
in the philosophy of Spinoza is found between the "substance" and its "attributes".[5]

Cordoveiro worked in close conjunction with his brother-
in-law Solomon Alkabetz, and like him belonged to the
ascetic religious community of the "Chaberim" (Associates),
for which he composed a set of rules.[6] As a specimen of
these we may quote the following : "Not to be betrayed
into anger, since anger delivers man into the power of
sin ; to associate on friendly terms with their fellow-men ;
to meet one of the Associates every day for the purpose
of discussing spiritual matters ; to review with an Associate
every Friday the actions of the week, and then prepare
for the reception of Queen Sabbath ; to confess their sins
before every meal and before going to sleep."

The leading figure of this circle was Isaac Luria, a
descendant of a learned German family, and known in
consequence as Ashkenazi (=German). The high esteem
in which he was held is shown by the fact that the whole
account of his life which has come down to us is legendary.[7]
He was born in 1534 in Jerusalem, but after his father's
death was brought up by an uncle in Cairo. By some
remarkable chance he obtained through a Marrano a copy
of the Zohar, and after reading it he spent thirteen years
as a hermit in a hut on the banks of the Nile preparing
himself for his mission. Every night his soul used to ascend
to heavenly spheres, where it was given the choice of the
divine lesson it would like to hear. A celestial guide was
assigned to him in the person of Simeon ben Yochai, who
ultimately advised him to settle in Safed. Here he was
soon followed by Chayim Vital from Damascus, who,
impelled by a dream, joined him "as his spiritual twin-
brother to teach whom he had come into the world". In
Safed, where he settled in 1570, Luria gathered round
himself a group of older and younger Cabbalists, who
looked upon him as their Master ; the association was, however, shortlived, since in 1572 he was carried off by a plague.

His activity was throughout purely personal and oral. The only writings ascribed to him were Hebrew explanations of the text of the Zohar and a commentary to the "Idroth", along with some hymns. Apart from this he wrote nothing, because he lived wholly in ineffable contact with realities. He is reported to have said himself: "I can hardly open my mouth without feeling as though the sea had burst its dams and overflowed."[7]

Our knowledge of the teachings of the Master is derived from the writings of his disciple Chayim Vital. He gave a new turn to the teaching of the Cabbalah, on the one hand through introducing important modifications in the doctrine of creation and world-order presented in the Zohar, on the other hand through concentrating attention on the striving of the soul for redemption. His theory of the soul was also in some respects peculiar.

The special primordial act of creation consists in "zimzum", a self-concentration of the divine life, through which an empty space is constituted within which it is possible for the world to unfold. The basis of the world is the "En-Sof" (Limitless), which first enters the category of actual existence in the form of light, as "Or En-Sof" (Light of the Limitless). The "Vessels" (Sefiroth) are not able to endure the inrush of the divine substance, and thus through the breaking of the "Vessels" (*shebirath hakelim, v.* Zohar I, 20a) a state of chaos is produced, along with the element of evil. In the centre of the created product stands the "Adam Kadmon", formed from the Sefiroth.

A special feature of the Lurian Cabbalah is the concept of "Parzufim" (Faces). This perhaps can best be understood from a remark at the opening of the "Book of Secrecy", according to which from a certain point of time onward the divine Countenances have always been turned towards one another (Zohar II, 176b). They were also explained as Sefiroth (or groups of Sefiroth) transplanted into the sphere of the human, or as forms of the human organism sublimated into the divine. The chief of them are the "Long of face", corresponding to the highest Sefirah, the "Short of face", corresponding to the middle Sefirah, and "Father and Mother", corresponding to Chokmah and Binah, while the cryptic term "Apple Garden" (Chakla di-Tappuchin) refers either to the general spiritual sphere common to these entities, or to the celestial home of the Messiah. These designations are taken from the Idroth, the Sifra di-Zeniuta, and other passages in the Zohar, e.g., II. 88a, from which the Lurian doctrine is directly derived.

An important place in the Lurian doctrine of the soul is occupied by the idea of "Gilgul", or transmigration, which is applied not only theoretically but also practically. The Master recognises the souls which he meets and can trace all the stages of their wanderings. "Looking at the forehead of a man he could tell at a glance from what particular source his soul was derived and the process of transmigration through which it had passed and what its present mission was on earth. . . . He was able to tell men their past as well as predict their future, and to prescribe for them the rules of conduct calculated to make amends for their shortcomings in a previous existence."[9]

Besides the regular reincarnation there are supposed to be exceptional cases of "soul pregnancy" (*Ibbur*). This takes place when either a soul of a deceased person which is already in a higher stage is attached to a soul still wandering on earth in order to support it, or when the former requires for its own perfection the co-operation of a human being still living on earth.

The Lurian teaching speaks also of "soul roots" (*sharashim*) and "soul sparks" (*nizozoth*). The former are common to a number of souls, and are particularly exemplified by the soul of Israel, though the soul of Cain is also an instance, while in Adam the souls of all men were combined. Soul sparks, which shoot off from the soul of a person, can be found not only in human beings, but also in other branches of animate and inanimate nature. In fact the whole of Nature seems to be peopled with spiritual beings. "He saw spirits everywhere, and heard their whispers in the rushing of the water, in the movement of the trees and grass, in the song or the twittering of the birds, even in the flickering of the flames."[10]

A similar train of thought produced the superstitious concept of the "Dibbuk", a kind of possession of a living person by the soul of a deceased person or by a demonic being ; similarly the belief in the existence of soul-elements in Nature also paved the way for the belief in demonic beings.

The Lurian mysticism is directed above all things to the perfection of the individual soul and the improvement of all worlds. Both endeavours are united in the idea of the "Tikkun" (improvement). There is a *tikkun* of souls, and even of dreams, and a *tikkun* of worlds ; the world of future perfection is itself called "Olam ha-tikkun" (world of *tikkun*).

Means of attaining perfection are asceticism and chastisements (*siggufim*), fasts (*taanioth*), and ablutions (*tebiloth*), as also special prayers and devotional exercises (*kawwanoth*), recited with close attention and with special watchfulness for mystical combinations of sounds ; when the purpose of these is to make contact with the name of God they are called "unions" (*yichudim*). Out of such prayers and meditations a special liturgy has been formed, to which belongs for instance the midnight prayer (*tikkun hazoth*, improvement of midnight), containing among other things elegies for Zion and readings from the Zohar. The "Prayer-book of Isaac Luria" was subsequently adopted by the Chassidim.

Certain special usages and customs were also current among the Safed Cabbalists, especially in the circle of Isaac Luria. The members of certain groups for instance publicly confessed their sins to one another on every Sabbath eve. The regular morning prayer was preceded by a devout union with the soul of all Israel. On the day before Sabbath Isaac Luria used to visit with his disciples the graves of the great Talmudic scholars in the neighbourhood

of Safed and Tiberias, in order to unite themselves with
their souls ; one was the grave of Simeon ben Yohai in
Meron.[11] On Sabbath he wore a white robe and partook
in a festal mood of the three Sabbath meals to which his
Sabbath hymns were dedicated.[12] In these the Sabbath
itself is introduced as a bride, reminding us of the popular
Sabbath song " Lechah Dodi ", which also had its origin
in Safed, being composed by Solomon Alkabetz. The
atmosphere of Safed in fact inspired a whole group of
poets,[13] including Israel of Nagara (1555-1628), whose
religious poems have an almost erotic character.

In the last resort all these practices were meant to
serve one end—" to hasten the coming of the Messiah."
There is a characteristic legend which relates that on one
Sabbath eve the Master asked the pupils whether they
desired to celebrate the Sabbath with him in Jerusalem,
and when they evinced doubt and hesitation he said that
that was the reason why they could not yet celebrate the
Messianic Sabbath.[14]

The personal activity of Isaac Luria, who reminded many
of his contemporaries of an ancient prophet, was confined
to the circle of his disciples. Already in his lifetime he
received the name of " the lion " or " the holy lion " (*ari
ha-kadosh*)[15] by which he has been subsequently known,
while his disciples were called the " lion's whelps " (*gure-
ha-aryeh*).

Under the influence of the new doctrines there arose
in Safed ascetic communities such as the already mentioned
" Chaberim ", also the " Tabernacle of Peace " (*Sukkath
Shalom*), for which Eliezer Askari wrote a " Book of the
Pious ", or more literally " Trembling " (*Sefer Haredim*).
A similar book " Commencement of Wisdom " (*Reshith
Chokmah*) was later adopted by the Chassidim.

Chayim ben Joseph Vital Calabrese (1542–1620)[16] completed the lifework of his master in various ways. He was
more of a visionary and wonder-worker, and more familiar
with occult knowledge. After the death of Isaac Luria he
considered it his chief task in life to put the latter's teaching

into writing. He kept his documents secret, however, until during an illness of his they were betrayed to the outer world. Later he returned to Damascus, where he died. On his deathbed he once more declared his writings to be the only authentic record of the teaching of his master.

His work has been preserved in a number of variants under the title " Ez Chayim " (Tree of Life), with the subtitle " Eight Gates ", a special chapter being devoted to the doctrine of transmigration. Another book of Chayim Vital, " Sha'are Kedushah " (Gates of Holiness), is a kind of guide for the development of the higher faculties.

Among others who were more or less closely connected with the Lurian circle in Safed[17] were Jacob Berab, Joseph Trani, Joseph Ashkenazi, Abraham ben Eliezer Halevi, who showed missionary zeal for the new teaching, Moses Galanti, Joseph Chagis, and the aged David ibn Zimra, who had been Isaac Luria's teacher in Cairo.[18] Among Luria's most prominent disciples were Joseph ibn Tabut and Israel Saruk.

From Palestine the revised Cabbalistic teachings were transplanted by a number of workers to Europe.[19] Conspicuous among these was the Marrano Jacob ben Chayim Zemach, who in 1619 came from Spain to Palestine, where he collected the writings of Chayim Vital, Meir Poppers from Prague, who put in order and revised these writings, and Nathan Spira-Ashkenazi,[20] from Cracow, who collected and edited the explanations of the prayers and the Kavvanoth. Israel Saruk disseminated the Cabbalah in Holland, and Menachem Azariah di Fano,[21] a disciple of Moses Cordoveiro, in Italy, which now as formerly served as a channel for the dissemination of Jewish mysticism. In Germany, Prague and Frankfort-on-Main became its centres, while in Poland the work of Nathan Spira and Isaiah ha-Levi Horowitz finally made this country the headquarters of the cultivation of the Cabbalah.

Prominent among these writers was Abraham Hereira,[22] a Marrano of Spanish birth, who derived his views directly

from Luria and less directly from the older Cabbalah and
religious philosophy, with a certain admixture of Platonic
philosophy. His work, " Sha'ar ha-Shamaim " (שער השמים
Gate of Heaven), written originally in Spanish and
later translated into Hebrew (and also into Latin), deals
chiefly with the problem of the original creation from the
" First Cause ", and propounds the view that the " air "
of the first-created already forms the being of the primordial
man, while the Sefiroth belong only to a second stage.
As with Cordoveiro, a central place is occupied in his system
by the contrast between the original spiritual unity and the
empirically given multiplicity.

Among the Cabbalists of Italy were further Moses
Zacuto[23] and, later, Immanuel Chai Ricchi,[24] who in his
book " Mishnath Chassidim " (The Mishnah of the Pious)
arranges the teaching of the Cabbalah in a system corresponding to that of the Mishnah. Thus to the order of
Seeds (Zera'im, i.e. agriculture) in the Mishnah correspond
cosmogony and metaphysics, to the Order of Festivals
the Kavvanoth, to the Order of " Women " (the laws
regulating the female life) the doctrines regarding the soul,
to the civil and criminal law those regarding demons and
" kelifoth ", to the Order of Kodoshim (sacrifices and
dedications) the teaching regarding Aziluth, and to the
Order of Tohoroth (purifications) the doctrines regarding
the three further stages of emanation.

Isaiah ha-Levi Horowitz systematised the whole field
of religious Judaism from the Cabbalistic point of view in
another, more popular form, and with such success that
his book " Shnei Luhoth Habrith " (The two Tables of
the Covenant) became the most widely read religious work
among the Jewish public, and he himself was called after
its first letters " the holy Sheloh ".[25]

The opposite line was taken by his nephew Sheftel
Horowitz, who in his book " Shefa Tal " (Abundance of
Dew, a pun on his own name), following in the footsteps
of the older Cabbalists, deals with the problem of Zimzum
and Aziluth, characterising the relation of the First Cause

to the First Effect as that of " Father " to " Son ", and with the Sefiroth, which also are regarded as having sprung from one another in the closest possible relationship of cause and effect.

Two of the most prominent Cabbalists of Poland next to those already mentioned were Matathias ben Solomon Delakrut,[26] who wrote commentaries to the works of older Cabbalists, and Samson of Ostropolie.[27]

Many Cabbalistic writings of this period display more strongly than those of previous ages the tendency to base the whole structure of Jewish religious life on the Cabbalah. Others again seek in the Cabbalistic tradition not a new religious experience, but only a starting-point for more or less philosophical disquisition, or a subject for rhetorical panegyric. This applies also to one of the latest and most attractive figures of the later Cabbalistic literature, Moses Chayim Luzzatto, who was born in Padua in 1707. When barely twenty years old Luzzatto gathered round himself a circle of young men (including students of Padua University) in order to communicate to them the revelations— partly Messianic—which he claimed to have received from a heavenly Maggid, who was even still speaking through his mouth, and from whose dictation he composed several writings. A letter of his which fell into the hands of the Rabbi of Altona, Moses Chagis, roused against him a storm of enmity from the side of the German and Italian Rabbis. In one of his controversies with the authorities he answered proudly : " I also have authority, the authority of the Lord, blessed be He, and of His Shekinah and all the members of the heavenly Academy." In the violent struggle which followed, Luzzatto, who was supported only by his teacher Isaiah Bassano, gave way step by step, until finally the ban was pronounced over the whole of his writings and he had to give a pledge not to publish any more without the approval of the Venetian Rabbis. Luzzatto thereupon gave up all aspirations in the field of the Cabbalah, and emigrated with his family to Amsterdam, and finally to Safed in Palestine, where in 1747 while on a visit to Acre he was like his master Isaac Luria carried off by a plague.[28]

The most important Cabbalistic writings of Moses Chayim Luzzatto are: "Choker u-Mekubbal" (Inquirer and Cabbalist), a dialogue between a rationalist and a student of the Cabbalah, intended as a polemic against the opponent of the Cabbalah, Leo de Modena; also an introduction to the Cabbalah, entitled "A hundred and thirty-eight Entrances to Wisdom". In addition a "second Zohar" had sprung from his youthful effusions. Drawing on a great store of Hebrew and secular knowledge, he also composed an ethical work entitled "Mesillath Yesharim" (Path of the Upright), a treatise on Logic and one on Rhetoric, and also several Hebrew dramas and numerous smaller poems (especially for festal occasions) which with their novelties of style and vocabulary exhibit this latest scion of the Cabbalists as the originator or first forerunner of the new-Hebrew poetry.

Luzzatto in his Cabbalistic writings claims for the Cabbalist a source of knowledge which is denied to the ordinary follower of Jewish tradition, while he distinguishes theoretical and practical Cabbalah from one another as being respectively the root and the branches of the sacred tree. The Cabbalah gives the answer to the two fundamental problems of religious philosophy—that of the origin of the finite creation in an infinite source and that of the origin of evil in the absolute good. Even the Cabbalah cannot penetrate to the ultimate source, but it can deal with the ten Sefiroth which, encircling one another like the skins of an onion, together constitute the world of emanation or the Adam Kadmon. Only in the last Sefirah, Malkuth (v. p. 96) does the supreme Will become manifest. Evil as the "Other side" (v. p. 99) has no existence in itself, but only so much as is given to it by the Good. On the ethical side the Cabbalistic system of thought leads to the ideal of the man who in the freedom of holiness is able to obtain the upper hand over the Other Side.[29]

In Palestine also there were notable Cabbalists after the golden age of Safed. One of them was Abraham Azulai,[30] author of a work " Chesed le-Abraham " (Love for Abraham), divided not into chapters but into " springs " and " brooks ", in which there is much discourse about the transmigration of souls. Still more important was Chayim ben Moses ibn Attar,[31] who lived on to the period of Chassidism, and whose commentary on the Pentateuch, " Or ha-Chayim " (Light of Life), was highly prized, especially by the Chassidim.

Among the later Cabbalists of Italy was also Joseph ben Immanuel Ergas of Livorno (born 1685, died 1730). He too composed a dialogue between a philosopher and a Cabbalist entitled " Shomer Emunim " (שומר אמונים) Protector of Faith), as also an introduction to the Cabbalah.

Finally as a last representative of the Cabbalah in Germany is to be mentioned Rabbi Nathan Adler (1741–1800), who spread the teachings of the Lurian mysticism among the numerous students of his Yeshibah, and practised ecstatic devotions, like the contemporary Chassidim. He was persecuted by the other Rabbis, but may have formed a link between cabbalistic and new-orthodox Judaism.

There were other writers also who, although not Cabbalists, showed a distinctly mystical trend in some of their works. Among these may be reckoned the celebrated Manasseh ben Israel,[32] who devoted a great part of his life to securing the return of the Jews to England, under the impulse of the Messianic idea that the gathering of Israel would have to be preceded by its dispersion over the whole earth. In his book " Nishmath Chayim " (Soul of Life) he has brought together material from the whole of Jewish literature, including the Cabbalah, as also from the teachings of Plato —often without much discrimination—to prove the divine nature of the human soul and its immortality. Along with him, although likewise no Cabbalist, may be mentioned the Prague scholar Judah Löwe ben Bezalel[33] (the " tall Rabbi Löw "), celebrated through his place in the

Golem legend, whose literary activity has not yet been adequately examined, but who seems to have been in touch with the alchemist circles of the Prague of that time.

During this period three of the originally esoteric doctrines of the Cabbalah found general acceptance with the mass of the people, profoundly affecting their outlook and way of life. These were the transmigration of souls, the impending advent of the Messiah, and the potency of certain magical formulæ.

1. The firm belief in the divine origin and goal of the human soul, in part also in its constant connection with God, is one of the pillars of the Jewish religion in general, and one of the principal themes of Jewish religious philosophy. From it sprang a conviction, which continually became stronger, of the continued existence of the soul after death. To this was added a further idea, first mentioned by the Gaon Saadiah as a doctrine, which was more closely defined in the Cabbalah and finally became generally accepted in Chassidism—the idea of the return of the soul to the body or reincarnation ; and this idea was supported by positive allegations of the incarnation of particular biblical and post-biblical personages.[34]

2. The expectation of a Messiah is an element of fundamental importance in all Jewish religious ideas concerning the future and final goal of the Jewish people and the world. The Messiah is regarded as on the one hand an eternal being who has even preceded the creation while on the other hand he is supposed not to reveal himself till the end of days (v. p. 116). Among the masses, it is true, the cosmic-religious notions, which are connected with that of the Shechinah, seem often to be lost in the national hope for deliverance from a constant state of exile and persecution. In particular, times of severe disillusionment and oppression were often marked by the appearance of so-called false Messiahs, the first classical example of which was given by Bar Cochba about eighty years after the destruction of the Second Temple.[35]   Again and again

many earnest inquirers, such as for instance the celebrated Isaac Abarbanel,[36] busied themselves with calculations of the time of deliverance on the basis of the prophecies of Daniel or other biblical passages, of historical comparisons concerning the duration of the exile, or of cabbalistic or astrological processes.

The most extensive and important of the Messianic movements in this period were those of Sabbatai Zevi and Jacob Frank,[37] in the 17th and 18th centuries respectively. The masses had been made highly receptive to these movements by the Messianic expectations implanted in them by the Lurian Cabbalah, itself an indication of an inner crisis, of a state of tension which went hand in hand with a profound change in Judaism itself. This tension, which probably reached its height in Poland,[38] was accentuated by Messianic calculations which fixed 1648 as the decisive year, though that year instead of deliverance brought the persecutions of Bogdan Chmielnitzky. None the less in the Sabbatian movement the immeasurable agony of the oppression was thrown off in an ecstatic outburst of wild enthusisam, blind obedience to a leader, and headstrong revolt against the rigid bonds of the law.[39] We are not surprised to find that in many cases Cabbalists were among the most ardent supporters of the new movement, and that followers of Sabbatai Zevi like Nathan of Gaza and Nehemiah Chiyun and Jacob Cardozo founded a new Cabbalah of Sabbatianism ; nor again that the two ecstatic movements, which each in its own way "abolished the Law ", in several cases led their followers to the two other religions of Christianity and Islam.

3. A belief in magic had already by underground channels penetrated deeply into the popular consciousness. An irrational faith in miracles gave rise to wonder cures both of a physical and a spiritual nature (e.g. expulsion of spirits), particularly to the use of half religious, half magical rites (*Segulloth*) for various occasions, to a high regard for sympathetic cures (*Refuoth*) and amulets (*Kemioth*), and

also to ceremonies and prayers tinged with magic, derived in part from the *Kavvanoth* of the Lurian Cabbalah (e.g., on New Year at the blowing of the Shofar, at the priestly blessing, etc.). Thus for instance it became customary to accompany the regularly prescribed prayer with longer prayers recited quietly (perhaps originally only meditated). The conflict over the practical Cabbalah with its wonder cures and its suspected adherence to Sabbatianism finally came to a head in the wearisome quarrel between the two great Rabbis of Altona, Jacob Emden and Jonathan Eibeschütz.[40]

NOTES TO CHAPTER VII.

[1] Joseph Caro was born in 1488 in Spain, from which country at the age of four years he emigrated with his father. He lived for some time in Adrianople, where he was head of a Yeshibah (talmudical school), and where at the age of 30 he composed his great halachic work "Bet Yosef", on which was based his shorter work, the "Shulchan Aruch". On the instruction of his heavenly mentor he migrated in 1535 to Safed, where he is said to have had many hundreds of disciples, and where he died in 1575 (i.e., after Isaac Luria). His book "Maggid Mesharim" was not published till after his death.

[2] Moses Alsheikh is reckoned as the most prominent preacher of the 16th century. He wrote among other things an allegorical-mystical commentary to the Bible, but was not included by Isaac Luria in the circle of his disciples.

[3] Moses Cordoveiro (ReMaK) lived from 1522 to 1570 in Safed. He wrote many works, among others " Or ne'erab ' (mixed light) as an introduction to the study of the Cabbalah. He died soon after the arrival in Safed of Isaac Luria, who at his burial saw two pillars of fire over his coffin.

[4] A still earlier encyclopædist of the Cabbalah was Meir ibn Gabbai, who was born in Spain in 1480. His system is contained in his work "Mar'oth Elohim" (visions of God), besides which he wrote on the Sefiroth and also mystical explanations of the liturgy. He compares the relation of God to the Sefiroth with that of the soul to the body. He calls the ten Sefiroth male emanations and the seven Hechaloth female, while man, according to him, unites in himself the radiations of all the Sefiroth. Like the Lurian Cabbalah after him, he lays special stress on the ideal of *Yichud*.

[5] *V.* S. Gelbhaus, " Die Metaphysik der Ethik Spinozas im Quellenlichte der Quabbalah ".

[6] *V.* Sol. Schechter, " Safed in the Sixteenth Century " (Studies in Judaism, II, 238, 239).

[7] These are contained in the popular " Shibche ha-Ari " (Eulogies of the Ari), as also in the response of Shlomele Dresnitz (*v.* note 17 *infra*).

[8] *V.* Sholem, Major Trends, etc., p. 250.

[9] *V.* Schechter, *op. cit.*, p. 265.

[10] *V.* Schechter, *op. cit.*, pp. 275, 276.   On definite incarnations of souls, portions of souls and soul sparks, *v. infra*, note 34 ; *cf.* also Schechter, *op. cit.*, pp. 276, 277.

[11] In Meron to this day on *Lag be-Omer* every year the " wedding-day ", i.e., the anniversary of the death, of Rabbi Simeon b. Yochai, is celebrated with bonfires and the singing of the hymn " Bar Yochai ".

[12] There is a German translation by the author in M. Zobel, " Der Sabbat ", also one by Meir Wiener in " Lyrik der Kabbalah ".

[13] Israel Nagara, b. 1535 in Safed, lived from 1579 in Damascus, and was finally Rabbi in Gaza, where he died in 1628.   He imitated Arabic and Spanish models both in religious and in secular erotic songs.

[14] The dangers arising from the magical tendencies in the Lurian Cabbalah were illustrated by the tragic end of Joseph della Reina, who, according to the story, by pushing his way forcibly into the highest spheres of existence, wished to hasten the coming of the Messiah.   The legend has been poetically treated by Meir Wiener in his poem " Messias ".

[15] A R I are the first letters of "̣ Ashkenazi Rabbenu Isaac ".

[16] Chayim Vital after the death of his master led a somewhat wandering life and among other things was for a time a Rabbi in Jerusalem.   A legendary account is given of his life also in the work " Shibche R. Chayim Vital ".

[17] The responsum of Shlomele Dresnitz, who came from Moravia to the Holy Land in 1603 (recently published in Ja'aris collection of Letters from Palestine), gives, long after the death of the Master, a still vivid picture of life in Safed, as he had been able to learn of it to some extent from the accounts of a later generation.   There were at that time in Safed still 18 talmudic colleges and 21 synagogues ; nevertheless religious life was already greatly on the decline.

[18] Solomo Molcho also (*v.* note 35 *infra*) had before the time of Isaac Luria lived for a while in Safed.

[19] On this point *v.* Philipp Bloch, " Die Kabbalah auf ihrem Hohepunkte und ihre Meister ".   *Cf.* also S. A. Horodetzky, " Mystisch-religiöse Strömungen unter den Juden in Polen im 16 bis 18 Jahrhundert ".

[20] He is the author of a well-known commentary on the Pentateuch, " Megalleh Amukoth " (Revealer of the Depths), and largely " conceived of the history of Israel as a world of soul-wanderings " (Horodetzky).

[21] Born 1548, died 1620 in Mantua.   He had many disciples from Italy and Germany, and composed " Ten Treatises " of a Cabbalistic character.

[22] Abraham (in Spanish, Alonzo de) Hereira died in 1631 in Amsterdam. The Latin translation of his work is to be found in Knorr von Rosen-roth's " Cabbala Denudata ".

[23] Moses ben Mordecai Zacuto (ReMeZ = Secret) was born about 1625 in Amsterdam.   He was probably a fellow-pupil with Spinoza in the Rabbinic school Ez Chayim.   At an early age he migrated to Posen. In Verona he became acquainted with a disciple of Chayim Vital, and thenceforward, as Rabbi and Revisor in Venice, Padua and Mantua, he devoted himself both as student and teacher to the Lurian Cabbalah, for the study of which he founded a seminary.   He died in 1697 in Mantua.   He composed responsa and discourses of a Cabbalistic character, a poem on the Inferno, and also a Hebrew drama.

[24] Immanuel Chai Ricchi was born in Ferrara. He led a life of many vicissitudes as Rabbi in Venice, Trieste, and other cities, and also lived several years in Safed. He died a violent death in Cento in 1743. Another work of his, "Maaseh Chosheb ", deals with the Tent of Meeting and its vessels.

[25] Isaiah Horowitz, born c. 1555 in Prague. As Rabbi of Posen and Cracow he was one of the leading personalities of Polish Jewry. He also lived for a time in Germany (Prague, Frankfort-on-Main) and in Palestine, where he died in 1630, in Safed. Of the life of his nephew Sabatai (Sheftel) Horowitz not much is known.

[26] Mattathias ben Solomon Delacrut lived about the middle of the 16th century, and finally settled in Italy. He wrote commentaries on astronomical and cabbalistic works, including Gikatilla's " Shaare Orah " (v. supra, p. 97).

[27] Simson ben Pesach Ostropolie, author of numerous cabbalistic writings, including " Dan Yadin " (He will surely judge), and " Likkute Shoshanim " (Bunch of Roses). He was a whole-hearted follower of Isaac Luria, was regarded as a miracle worker and devoted himself entirely to preparing for the coming of the Messiah time. He regarded the Cabbalah as so holy that he considered the disclosure of many of its secrets to be dangerous. He died as a martyr in the persecutions of Chmielnitzky, being murdered in a synagogue where he was praying with three hundred others.

[28] The life and works of Luzzatto are described in detail in the monograph of S. Ginzburg, who has also discovered many new letters to and from Luzzatto.

[29] Ginzburg rightly points out that the ideal of the " holy man " set forth by Luzzatto is closely akin to the Chassidic conception of the Zaddik (v. p. 142).

[30] Born in 1570 in Fez. He migrated at an early age to Palestine, where he lived for many years in Gaza and died in Hebron. The well known biographer Chayim Joseph David Azulai was descendant of his.

[31] He also came from Morocco, where he was born in 1696. He went, however, at an early age to Palestine, where he was honoured as a saint and devoted his whole life to study and mystical meditation, dying in Jerusalem in 1748.

[32] Manasseh ben Israel was born in 1604 in Lisbon. He gave up his Rabbinate in Amsterdam in order to go to London, where he stayed for two years, during which he had close political connections with Cromwell. He died in 1657 in Middelburg, while on his way back from England to Amsterdam. He carried on an extensive correspondence with Christian scholars, and was friendly with Rembrandt, who painted his portrait. His work " Esperanza d'Israel " in which he expressed his messianic faith, won great celebrity. His activities in England have been described by M. Kayserling, Lucien Wolf and Cecil Roth.

[33] Judah Löwe ben Bezalel was born in Posen and died in 1609 in Prague. He was alternately Rabbi in Posen and in Prague, where he founded a celebrated talmudical school, the " Klaus "; for a time he was also chief Rabbi of Moravia (at Nikolsburg). His writings include " Netiboth Shalom " (Paths of Peace), a kind of manual of Jewish ethics, a super-commentary on Rashi's commentary on the Pentateuch, " Nezach Yisrael " (Victory of Israel), a mystical (and messianic) apology for Judaism, and notes on the Passover Hagadah.

He is one of the few Rabbis to whom a monument has been erected, the donors in his case being the Czech Government.

[34] Thus according to Jewish legends and traditions we have the reincarnation of Aaron the High Priest in Eli and Ezra; of Cain in Jethro the "Kenite"; of Abel in Moses; of Jacob in Mordecai; of Laban in Nabal; of Phineas in Elijah, and of Tamar in Ruth. Moses appears again in Simeon b. Yochai and later in Isaac Luria. The soul of Chayim Vital was reckoned as one which had not been affected by the sin of Adam; it was, nevertheless, overshadowed by the soul of Rabbi Akiba. The name ADaM was also explained as a *notarikon* of Adam, David, Messiah (*v.* L. Bendavid).

[35] Already in the time of the Second Temple, when Judæa became a Roman province, Theudas claimed to be a Messiah. In the 8th century Serene proclaimed himself Messiah with the object of driving the Mohammedans out of Palestine. The appearance of false Messiahs (one of whom was David Alroy) became more frequent in the epoch of the Crusades. The fateful period after the expulsion of the Jews from the Pyrenean peninsula is marked by the appearance of David Reubeni (subject of a novel by Max Brod) and Shlomo Molcho. One reason why the Lurian Cabbalah cherished the belief in the Messianic advent with such intensity was that Isaac Luria, who thought that he felt in himself the soul of the Messiah son of Joseph, declared that secrets might now be revealed because the days of the Messiah were near. And Chayim Vital wrote in his *Ez Chayim* that through the study of the Cabbalah the coming of the Messiah would be hastened. For further details see A. H. Silver, "A History of Messianic Speculation in Israel".

[36] Isaac Abravanel was born in 1437 in Lisbon. He was for a time Financial Minister to the King of Portugal, but was accused of a conspiracy and forced to leave Portugal, from where he fled to Toledo. He was a victim of the expulsion from Spain, of which he gives an account in one of his commentaries. After many wanderings he at length settled in Venice, where he entered into the service of the Republic, and died in 1508. His Bible commentaries were celebrated, and brought him into contact with Christian theologians, against whom he upheld the Jewish doctrine of the Messiah. His Messianic views are contained chiefly in his commentary on the Book of Daniel. In general he sought to effect a synthesis between cabbalistic and rationalistic tendencies.

[37] On Sabbatai Zevi see especially the artistic character sketch by Joseph Kastein. On Frank and the Frankists see the monograph of the historian Grætz. Much material on both movements is contained in David Kahane's "History of the Cabbalah (Cabbalists, Sabbatians, and Chassidim)", in Hebrew. *V.* Index.

[38] *V.* S. A. Horodetzky, "Mystisch-religiöse Strömungen unter den Juden in Polen im 16–18 Jahrhundert".

[39] In order to justify the often pathological conduct of their so-called "Messiah", these men stamped blasphemies and sacrileges as holy acts, and proclaimed the dangerous doctrine that in order to combat evil it is necessary for man to enter into sin.

[40] On this conflict see the accounts in the Histories of Grætz and Dubnow, and also the above-mentioned work of David Kahane. The Cabbalistic teaching of Jonathan Eibeschütz is to be found in Isak Mieses, "Darstellung der jüdischen Geheimlehre".

VIII

CHASSIDISM

AMONG the by-products of the study of the Cabbalah in the later Middle Ages was the appearance in Europe, in the sixteeneth century and later, of a number of men who professed to be able by means of the Divine Name to work wonders and who in consequence were known to the Jewish public by the title of *Baal-Shem* (Master of the Name). Thus there was a Baal-Shem named Elia of Chelm in the 16th century, and two men named Joel Heilprin bore the title in Ostrog and Satanov respectively in the 17th and 18th centuries. There were several Baale-Shem in Germany —e.g. Elia Loans in the 16th century, and R. Săckel Wormser, the Baal-Shem of Michelstadt, 1769–1847. There was also a Baal-Shem in London, Chayim ben Samuel Jacob Falk[1] (1708–1782), who was said to have saved a great synagogue in a fire. It is a significant fact, due largely to psychological reasons, that most of these emerged and exercised their influence chiefly in the East of Europe— Poland, Volhynia, Podolia, Bukovina, White Russia, and Lithuania. It would seem that in these districts, after the Chmielnitzky persecutions, the echoes of the older Cabbalah combined with the tragic collapse of the pseudo-Messianic movements to implant a strong mystical yearning in the Jewish population,[2] which found vent among other things in a belief in these professing wonder-workers. Another product of the same yearning was the rise in Poland at the turn of the 17th and 18th centuries of a movement the adherents of which called themselves Chassidim. They consisted partly of former followers of Sabbatai Zevi, and about 120 of them under the leadership of Judah ha-Chassid and Chayim Malach from Kielce started out on a migration to the Holy Land, which, however, came to a tragic end.[3]

Historically by far the most important of these " Baale-Shem ", and the only one who struck out a new line of religious development, was Israel ben Eliezer Shem-tob, commonly known simply as Baalshem, or by the still shorter name Besht.[4] He was born in 1700 in Okup, on the border of Volhynia and Podolia, and spent more of his childhood in the solitude of the woods than in the children's school the " cheder ". At the age of twelve, however, he hired himself to the village teacher as an assistant (Behelfer). " Thereupon the inhabitants of the sleepy village witnessed a wonderful change. Israel led every day a procession of singing children through the streets to school and took them by a roundabout way through meadows and woods back to their homes. No more did the children show pale drooping faces as before. They shouted for joy and carried flowers and green boughs in their hands " (Buber). As porter of the Beth-hamidrash the boy received secret writings from the son of Rabbi Adam, who had assigned them to him on his death.[5] Unknown, in the guise of an ignorant rustic, of whom his learned brother-in-law Gershon Kutower from Brody was ashamed, he spent several years in lowly occupations, such as keeping an inn for peasants, which was managed by his wife while he himself lived in a hut in the woods, where he buried himself in thought, only coming home on Sabbaths. Gradually, however, he revealed his wonderful nature to a few of his visitors, and finally to a pupil of his brother-in-law, who spread the report in the town. Thereupon the Baalshem one day while halfway through the wood met a crowd of followers who made for him a throne of boughs and hailed him as Master. During the next few years he wandered about,[6] finally settling in Miedzyborz near Brody, where he died in 1760.

Like Isaac Luria in the 16th century, Israel Baalshem gathered round him a circle of disciples who regarded him as a holy man and a wonder-worker, and who followed his guidance implicitly. He wrote even less than Luria and exercised his influence almost wholly by oral teaching. This teaching, like Luria's, was based on the Cabbalah. But whereas Luria struck out new lines both in the theoretical and the practical Cabbalah, Israel Baalshem was an innovator only on the practical side. He contributed little to Jewish mystical thought ; his importance lay in the fact that he introduced a new application of mysticism to life and conduct. This new way of life was chiefly distinguished by its demonstrative piety, and for this reason no doubt his followers adopted the name of Chassidim, or pietists.[7]

The more important decendants of the Baalshem were his two grandsons, Moses Ephraim and Baruch of Miedzyborz, and his famous great-grandson, Nachman of Bratzlaw.[8] But his real spiritual heir, and the centre of the Chassidic movement after his death, was Dob Beer of Mezric (died in 1772), also called the " Great Maggid ", in virtue of his popularity as a religious preacher (*Maggid*). Dob Beer became the founder of another line which is of great importance for the inner history of Chassidism. He had a son Abraham (d. 1776), known on account of his unworldly purity as " Mal'ach " (Angel). His son Shalom Shachna displayed even in his appearance the dignity of a Zaddik. Finally, Shalom's son, Israel of Rushin (the " Rushiner "),[9] became the prototype of the wonder-working Rabbi and the founder of the " Dynasties " of Sadagora and Czortkow. (His sons were Abraham Jacob Friedmann, Nahum of Stepinesht, and David Moses of Czortkow.)

Most of the leading figures in Chassidism were actually members of the circles of the Baalshem or the Great Maggid, or their descendants. The most prominent disciples of the Baalshem were, next to Dob Beer of Mezric and Jacob Joseph of Polna (or Zarygorod), the Lithuanian Pinchas of Koretz, who was regarded by the Baalshem more as a friend than as a disciple, and Jechiel Michael of Zlocow (d. 1781 or 1782), and the latter's son Wolf of Zbaraz and pupil Meir of Przemysl. Among the disciples of the Great Maggid were Menahem Mendel of Vitebsk (d. 1781), Samuel Schmelke of Nikolsburg (d. 1778) and his disciple Moshe Leib of Sassow ; also Aaron of Karlin, Nahum of Chernobyl, Abraham Kalisker (once a disciple of the Vilna

Gaon, the great Talmudist), Levi Yizhak of Berditchev, Sussye of Hanipol (d. 1800), his brother Elimelech of Lizensk and the latter's disciple Menahem Mendel of Rymanov; finally the great Shneur Zalman of Ladi (d. 1813), Israel of Koznitz (the "Koznitzer Maggid"), Solomon Karlin and his disciple Uri of Strelisk, surnamed the "Seraph", and Jacob Yizchak of Lublin (d. 1816). The successors of the last-named were Jacob Yizchak (d. 1814) and his disciple Simcha Bunem of Przysucha, Naphtali of Ropczyce, and Zewi Hirsch of Zydaczow.[10]

In modern Chassidism (as distinguished from the German medieval movement of the same name, v. p. 71), the strong mystical exercise of the will power which is the characteristic of the Lurian Cabbalah is in some respects carried to still further lengths, though in others it is somewhat relaxed. There is the same religious fervour as in the Lurian system, but the gloomy asceticism of that movement disappears, and is replaced by a willingness to accept thankfully the earthly boons of life also. In Chassidism too the tendency noted in the last chapter to permeate the whole of the religious life with mystical elements reaches its full development.

This tendency was accompanied in Chassidism by an extreme popularisation of mysticism. Whereas all earlier Cabbalistic activities had been conducted by solitary inquirers or esoteric groups, the new movement, especially in its inception, appealed specifically to the simple people.[11] In Chassidism esoteric research and training receded into the background in face of an illumination which was kindled and maintained by direct contact with external life. Martin Buber, it is true, underestimates the spiritual achievement of Cabbalism when he sees in Chassidism a "desystematising of the mystery" (Entschematisierung des Mysteriums). Still, it is the fact that on the whole it did not reach the spiritual level of the old methods of esoteric inquiry and was indeed almost ignorant of those methods; and it would seem that the outer descent to the masses, while it carried mysticism into the whole of the religious life, was accompanied by an inner descent from the highest spheres of thought into the denser atmosphere of religious emotionalism. Hence the main characteristic of Chassidism is to be found in a religious *feeling* which penetrates the whole of being and governs the whole of life, from its profoundest concerns to its most trivial.

It is sometimes said that in Chassidism the Messianic idea receded into the background. This is correct if by that idea we understand the tense and hourly expectation of the Messiah, with the overpowering desire " to hasten the end ". To a certain extent—and this is perhaps the essential difference between the Chassidic and the Lurian mysticism—the moment itself is fulfilment, containing some element of Messianism. Nor is there any contradiction between this attitude and the continual readiness for the Messiah, of which we sometimes hear.[12]

This attitude springs from the feeling, which is of central importance in Chassidism and was sedulously cultivated by it, of a profound rejoicing in God, a rejoicing which manifested itself outwardly also and which rejected ascetism on principle, since by comparison with it all sadness appeared as an obstacle to the *élan* of the soul.[13] This joy has its root in the inner fervour (Hithlahabuth) which springs only from the deepest religious emotion, and which when heightened into the state of ecstasy can bring about complete self-effacement (*Bittul ha-yesh*, elimination of the individual existence).

Chassidism laid more stress than the theoretical—and even more than the practical—Cabbalah on the actual consummation of the religious life. The Chassid effected this through the medium of " service " (Avodah), which was at once service of God and daily work, but which in either case derived its whole significance from the spiritual intention, " Kavvanah ". The concept of *kavvanah* in Chassidism is somewhat different from what it is in the Lurian mysticism ; it signifies less an effort of the will centred on the attainment of a definite end than the purposeful direction of the whole being in accordance with some feeling springing from the depths of one's nature. This is mirrored in the true Chassid in the virtue of humility (*Shifluth, Anvah*), which springs alike from man's connection with the lower worlds and his vision of the higher worlds.[14] A certain laxity in religious practice arose from the fact that in the intensity of religious feeling the prescribed times for prayer were not always strictly observed ; it is in fact related of many of the Chassidic leaders that they were often so taken up with putting themselves in the right frame of mind that they missed the proper time for beginning the prayer. Even more important was the ecstatic devotion with which the prayer itself was offered ; this could be so intense that, for instance, one of the masters (Elimelech of Lizensk) had to look at the clock while praying in order to remind himself that he was in the temporal world.

Characteristic of the Chassidic way of life were also a fondness for external nature, and the creation of a special religious-popular music, the favourite pieces of which were first a melody of Shneur Zalman, and then the airs of the " Tolna Maggid ". This music was closely connected with the religious male dance,[15] which gave the most marked expression to the ecstatic sense of religious comradeship.

There were many respects in which Chassidism burst through the bonds of tradition, in none more completely than the relation, half religious, half social, of leader and community. The striving of Chassidism for a closely-knit communal life on a religious basis was focused in the dominating figure of the " Zaddik " (Righteous Man). Personally the Zaddik led the life of a saint, while in relation to the three groups of disciples, community, and pilgrims, he not only fulfilled the function of a religious leader, but at the same time was the embodiment of a higher power gifted with mystical insight, superior intelligence, and worldly wisdom, which enabled him to intervene with effect in human affairs.

The teachings of Chassidism, as we find them in the utterances of the Baalshem and in the writings of his disciples, contain no new ideas of importance which are not already found in the Cabbalah, only they lay more emphasis on the practical side of the individual life.

The omnipresence of God is taught with almost pathetic insistence. It is the duty of man to serve God with every one of his movements (Pinchas of Koretz). The body of man is only an outer robe, his essence lies in the world of thought, in which it is his task to release the hidden " sparks ", that is, to bring them back to their pure source. The most holy action is that of prayer, the main concern of which is not the individual need, but the exile and deliverance of the Shechinah. In the scheme of being evil also has its place as the throne of the good, and for this reason it is man's duty to serve God also with the evil inclination, which he thereby transforms (Jacob Joseph). The " pious " of the generation are the soul of the people and of the age. Those who relieve them of material cares, so that they can devote themselves wholly to their spiritual work, are compared to the " bearers of the holy ark ".

Chassidism was reduced to a systematic doctrine only in the comparatively rationalistic Lithuania, in the form of the so-called " Chabad " founded by Shneur Zalman.[16] This word is formed from the initial letters of the Sefiroth-trinity : Chochmah, Binah, Daath (v. p. 96). The doctrine of the Chabad is presented in the " Sefer Tanya " (Book of Teaching), or " Likkute Amarim " (Collection of Sayings) of the founder, which was widely read, and also in other writings of Shneur Zalman. It is made up of ideas concerning God, the soul, and the religious life. The doctrine of the soul is worked out in greater detail than the others. While in virtue of its origin the soul is of immutable nature, yet there dwell in the human nature two souls, a heavenly and a physical, of which the former has its abode in the head and in the right chamber of the heart, and the latter in the left chamber. These two souls are in continual conflict with one another. Each of them has ten divisions, and the basic faculties of the soul correspond to the Sefiroth.

Thus to Chesed corresponds piety, to Geburah control of the feelings, to Rachamim (v. p. 96) a balance between the two. The second or animal soul is impelled to sin by the body, but this does not exonerate man, since he is a free being. A distinction is further made between natural qualities of the soul and those which are determined and ruled by the reason, and within the good qualities again between those in which the bad are subjected to the good and those in which the bad is transformed into the good, e.g. bodily desire into the desire to serve God. Purification of the soul is achieved in a threefold manner—through thought, word, and action, especially by subjecting them to the influence of religion. In particular the teaching and the whole outlook of the " Rav of Reussen ", as Shneur Zalman was called, has as its object to reconcile the Cabbalah with Rabbinism. It was no accident that along with commentaries on the Bible he also composed explanations of the Zohar, and drew frequently from Isaac Luria. He also composed a Chassidic prayer-book, and, at the request of the " Great Maggid ", a Chassidic Shulchan Aruch.

In the Chassidic tradition individual Masters are distinguished by the special emphasis which they laid on particular qualities or activities. Thus Levi Yizhak of Berditchev, who on account of his great popularity was known simply as " the Berditchever ", was noted for a crude ecstatic piety which expressed itself particularly in his vehement style of praying ; this was frequently accompanied by childish wrangling with " the All-Merciful ", or even by exclamations in the vernacular. The child-like Sussye of Hanipol was so self-effacing as to become impervious to bodily suffering, while on the other hand he was tender with sinners to the point of taking their guilt on himself. Samuel Schmelke, who was Rabbi in a distant town of Moravia, was a master of the religious discourse. The " Koznitzer Maggid " showed a heroic disregard of physical pain and was wonderfully effective in rousing the congregation to prayer. Moshe Leib of Sassow was the exponent of helpful and sympathetic love. The " Lubliner " Jacob Yizchak of Lublin, also called "our holy Rabbi", (Rabbenu ha-kodosh) was known as a "seer", while his disciple Jacob Yizhak of Przysucha was called simply the " Jew " (Yehudi). Abraham Malach presents us with an example of heavenly purity, while Löbl Soreh's (= Sarah's) was a wonder-worker who, as one of the legendary " thirty-six saints " of the generation, laboured quietly in secret. There was also a female Zaddik—the Maid of Ludomir (the " Ludmirer Moid ")—to whom a special group of Chassidim attached themselves.

The new movement wrought deep and, in its early stages, beneficial changes in Jewish life and outlook. Under its influence the arid disputatiousness of Talmudic learning gave place to simplicity of expression and fervour of faith ; the tendency to self-mortification receded before the recognition that the soul can endure the body and has no need to separate from it (Dob Beer of Mezric) ; the spirit of censoriousness was replaced by one of sympathy and indulgence (Abraham Joshua of Apt) ; and official pomp and show were discarded in favour of a dignified simplicity in public appearances (Aaron of Karlin). Unfortunately the teaching of Chassidism soon degenerated into an obscurantism which retained the worst features of Rabbinism without its redeeming intellectuality, while the institution of the Zaddik produced a number of wonder-Rabbis each holding his own court and imposing on the credulity of his followers. Efforts were made to bring back Chassidism, thus early threatened with petrification, to ·the original sources of mysticism and to the paths of simple virtue. These efforts were particularly marked in the Chabad society, founded by Shneur Zalman. They also led to the clothing of the esoteric teaching of Chassidism in allegorical stories, like those of Rabbi Nachman Bratzlaw, which in their descriptions of spiritual and psychical experiences has no special connection with traditional Judaism.[17]

The spread of the Chassidic movement caused a profound schism in the Jewry of East Europe. Springing as it did from a positive impulse to reawaken religious feeling, it acted as a challenge to Rabbinic Judaism which was threatening to fall a prey to a rigid legalistic formalism, a soulless study of the Talmud, and a blind exaltation of learning. In the more southern districts Chassidism was allowed to unfold itself at first without let or hindrance, but it aroused strong opposition as soon as it crossed the boundaries of Lithuania,[18] where small communities were formed in Minsk, Sklow, and Vilna.

The opponents, who received the name of "Mithnagedim" (the exact equivalent of "Protestants") ranged themselves for the most part under the ægis of the greatest Talmudic authority of the day, the "Gaon" Elijah ben Solomon of Vilna. The Chassidim at first adopted a yielding attitude ; they repeatedly offered to submit their views to public discussion, and in certain individual cases submitted to severe humiliations, such as flogging. None the less in the winter of 1772 a sentence of excommunication was pronounced against the new "sect" ; notice of it was sent far and wide by means of official letters, and it was even repeated in many Jewish centres such as Brody in East Galicia. The first literary rejoinder from the Chassidic side was made in the year 1781 with the pamphlet "Toldoth Yakob Yosef " by Jacob Joseph of Polna, in which the corruptions of Talmudism were sharply criticised. Thereupon the excommunication was pronounced again in a stronger form with great pomp and ceremony at the fair of Selwe ; this time it was applied also to the personal and business interests of the persons affected, and threatened to cut off the Chassidim not only as before from all public religious activity, but also from all possibilities of making a living. The struggle which followed, and which was accompanied among other things by holocausts of books, was conducted on both sides with great bitterness. Among the reproaches hurled at the Chassidim, and on account of which they were stigmatised as enemies of the Jewish community, were laxity in observing the proper times of prayer, arbitrary alterations in ceremonial and liturgy (including the introduction of the Lurian prayer-book), and above all the ecstatic and noisy character of their religious and communal life, by which the " Karliner " were especially distinguished.

The leading Chassidim in Lithuania and White Russia were first and foremost the pacific Shneur Zalman in Lozno, then Israel Polocker and Menahem Mendel of Vitebsk. The last-named, in order to avoid all quarrelling, emigrated in 1777 along with Abraham Kalisker and Israel Polocker to the Holy Land, where they settled with about 300 persons in Safed. Among the mithnagdic opponents the lead was taken by the Brisk Rabbi Abraham Katzenellenbogen.

Political activities were also brought into this struggle.[19] The first excommunication took place in the year of the first partition of Poland, and the Chassidim are said to have won over the new Russian authorities at first for their cause.

The struggle reached its climax in 1797. After pronouncing a new sentence of excommunication against the Chassidim—this time provoked by themselves—the Vilna Gaon died suddenly during the festival of Sukkoth, and the Chassidim organised celebrations of rejoicing at the hour of his burial, which led to violent encounters. Everyone who even supported the Chassidim was now declared an enemy of Judaism. The Mithnagedim also obtained greater influence with the authorities, and they succeeded twice in having the " Rav of Reussen ", whom they denounced as a Freemason, imprisoned. Eventually, however, the Government convinced itself of the harmlessness of the whole movement, and in 1800 the " sect of the Chassidim " was recognised as lawful.

A new opposition movement to Chassidism soon arose from the opposite side—from the Jewish Enlightenment movement, the representatives of which, following the lead of Moses Mendelssohn, sought to absorb into Judaism European, and particularly German, culture, and from which sprang—particularly in East Europe—the great Haskalah movement,[20] with Hebrew for its literary language.

How the followers of this movement regarded Chassidism
may be seen from the fact that the Kantian Solomon
Maimon, who went from Poland to Berlin, in his auto-
biography has little more to relate of the Chassidim than
instances of childish superstition, which no doubt he had
observed personally.

The conflict between Haskalah and Chassidism belongs
to the second phase of the history of the Chassidic movement, when an approximation to Rabbinism, combined
with mystical superstition and a degrading cult of the
" Zaddikim ", had almost completely effaced the original
character of the movement or even turned it into its
opposite. Hence the leaders of the Haskalah movement
(e.g. Joseph Perl, Isaac Baer Levinsohn, and the satirist
Isaac Erter) had little but ridicule for the Chassidic way
of life. An exception, however, is to be found in the work
of Eliezer Zweifel, " Shalom al Yisrael " (Peace upon
Israel). Some of the leaders themselves also found the
obscurantism of the movement more than they could stomach
in the modern world. In such figures as Baer of Sadagora,
one of the six sons of the Rushiner, and Mendel of Kock,
we see the results of a tragic internal struggle with the
spirit of the age, the former having for a time crossed over to
the Maskilim, while the latter, after being for a time a strict
follower of the Talmud, at length openly repudiated the Law.

Chassidism, so long as it was living, penetrated much
more than Rabbinism into the soul of the Jewish masses
of Eastern Europe. Thus the Chassidic " Rebbe ", in contrast with the mithnagdic " Rav ", was, in spite of his
elevation as a saint and wonder-worker, completely a man
of the people. His faithful followers visited him at least
once a year in order to obtain assistance and advice in
regard to material and spiritual problems, and on such
occasions enjoyed the stirring experience of hearing Torah,
i.e. religious wisdom, from the mouth of the Zaddik at the
third Sabbath meal, called " Melaveh Malkah " (escort
of the Queen). The Chassidim themselves formed a
fraternal community, the members of which met at fixed

places of prayer (the "Klaus") and joined together in prayer, song, and dancing.

One feature of the Chassidic life seems especially to have contributed to its degeneration. Even the first masters attached particular value to the sanctification of the natural impulses, e.g. to the partaking with joy of the holy meals. The lofty idea of releasing by this means the sparks of the soul exiled into the external world was not always understood by the rank and file of the Chassidim, and this in many cases gave rise to an unhealthy mixture of religious devotion with physical indulgence.

A certain revival of Chassidism—more reminiscent than actual—was brought about by the rediscovery of Jewish vital forces and the affectionate study of the soul of the Jewish people which marked the Jewish renaissance movement, as embodied in the new Hebrew and new Yiddish literature. Above all J. L. Perez in his tales and sketches illustrated with wonderful power the life of the Jewish people as shaped internally by the forces of Chassidism. In his drama "Die Goldene Keit" (the Golden Chain) he traces through four generations the decline from the saintly fanatic who dreams of the coming of the Eternal Sabbath, through the doubter and the hypocrite to the modern sceptic. In Hillel Zeitlin we find a certain renewal of the inner world of Chassidic thought and feeling combined with a modern outlook. And the dramatist S. Anski (S. S. Rapaport) draws from Chassidic traditions rich material for psychological analysis.[21] Among the many historical and literary works dealing with the subject special mention should be made of those of Martin Buber, who both as religious thinker and as artist has made the inner history of Chassidism and its chief representatives familiar to wide circles of readers.

This brings us to the immediate present—the present of various new tendencies in Judaism, above all the national and Zionist, the present of the most terrible persecutions of the whole of Jewish history, the present of the deepest inner convulsions. The conflicts which are raging in the soul, the experiences which are being stored up by the mind at this moment have as yet found no expression, much less shaped themselves into a movement. On the question whether and how this can be done may depend the continuation and renovation of Judaism. A survey of the history of Jewish mysticism in the past is one of the most important preliminaries for the performance of this task.

NOTES TO CHAPTER VIII.

[1] Falk came originally from Poland. He was said to have saved himself by the use of magic from the stake in Westphalia, and settled in 1742 in London, where he became acquainted with prominent Freemasons and with the Duke of Orleans. He is said to have gone about with a fantastic parade and was regarded also by non-Jews, who called him " Chief of all the Jews ", as a kind of magician. He was connected with another wonder-worker, the Baal-Shem of Podjaice, Rabbi Moses David.

[2] V. S. A. Horodetzky, " Mystisch-religiöse Strömungen unter den Juden in Polen ".

[3] V. Horodetzky, op. cit., pp. 59–63.

[4] The chief source for the life of the Baalshem is the collection of legends about him known as " Shibche ha-Besht " (Eulogies of the Besht) by an anonymous author, in Hebrew and Yiddish. We have also " Kether Shem Tob " (Crown of a good name), containing sayings of the Baalshem ; " Zawaath ha-Besht " (Testament of the Besht), and some original letters.

[5] According to Sholem (" Major Trends in Jewish Mysticism ", pp. 327, 328) the mysterious designation Rabbi Adam hides the historical figure of a Sabbatian, Rabbi Heschel Zoref of Vilna, since we know from documentary evidence that a manuscript written by him came after his death into the hands of the Baalshem.

[6] There seems to be some ground for the statement made in the biographies of the Baalshem that he once embarked with his daughter on a pilgrimage to the Holy Land, where he wished to meet the Cabbalist Chayim ibn Attar. Fate, however, decided otherwise, and he was prevented from reaching his goal by a disturbance either of the elements or of his own mind. The great-grandson of the Baalshem, Nachman of Bratzlaw, also undertook a journey to Palestine, which was rendered very adventurous by the campaign of Napoleon which took place at that time.

[7] The most important recent accounts of Chassidism are those by S. Dubnow in " Geschichte des Chassidismus " (Hebrew and Russian : German translation by A. Steinberg) ; Ahron Marcus (Verus) in " Der

Chassidismus " (1888), containing much material but not well arranged ; S. A. Horodetzky (Hebrew); David Kahane (Hebrew); Martin Buber, who has thrown into artistic form and interpreted a great part of the Chassidic tradition; and Paul Levertoff, who brings into relief the points of resemblance between Chassidism and Christianity. There are also monographs by Schechter, Bogratschoff, Sol. Birnbaum (on the Baalshem), Chayim Bloch, and others. Martin Buber's " Legende des Baalshem " has been translated into English under the title of " Jewish Mysticism and the Legend of Baalshem ". A full exposition of the teaching of Chassidism, drawn from all the sources, is contained in Louis Newman's " The Chassidic Anthology ".

[8] For Nachman of Bratzlaw's works and the literature about him see S. A. Horodetzky, " Nachman von Bratzlaw ", M. Buber, " Die Geschichten des Rabbi Nachman ", and a bibliography by G. Sholem.

[9] Because of the princely state which he maintained, Israel of Rushin became suspect to the Russian Government, and when two Jewish informers were killed he was kept for a long time in prison. In 1840, in order to escape persecution, he removed to Austria, finally settling in Sadagora in the Bukovina.

[10] For the succession of Chassidic Masters see Buber, " Die Chassidischen Bücher ", pp. 705–709.

[11] This is shown among other things by the extent to which Yiddish is used in the Chassidic literature.

[12] R. Moses Teitelbaum awaited the coming of the Messiah every moment. When he heard a noise in the street he asked with a trembling voice " Has the messenger appeared ? " Before he went to sleep he laid out his Sabbath clothes next to his bed and put his pilgrim's staff on them. A watcher was engaged to wake the Rabbi at the first sign that he perceived (Buber, " Das verborgene Licht," in " Die Chassidischen Bücher ", p. 651).

[13] *Cf.* the saying of Jacob Joseph of Polna : " The Shechinah is drawn down from heaven not through sadness but through joy in the fulfilment of the precepts."

[14] *V.* " Das Leben der Chassidim " in Buber's " Die Legende des Baalshem " (" Die chassidischen Bücher," pp. 134–164).

[15] Chassidic dances have in recent times frequently been introduced on the stage in Jewish dramas, e.g. by Peretz and Anski.

[16] Shneur Zalman ben Baruch was from Ladi, hence known as the " Rav of Ladi ". Having accompanied Menachem Mendel of Vitebsk as far as Mohilev on his pilgrimage to the Holy Land, he settled in that town, and afterwards in Ladi. He died in 1812 during his flight from the army of Napoleon. On his part in the Chassidic struggles, *v.* p. 147.

[17] Other leading contributors to Chassidic literature are Jacob Joseph of Polna (" Toledoth Ya'kob Yosef "), Pinchas of Koretz, Nachum of Chernobyl, and Elimelech of Lizensk.

[18] The conflicts between Chassidim and Mithnagedim are described in detail in S. Dubnow's " History of Chassidism ".

[19] Among the strangest stories in the political records of Chassidism is that of the occult influence said to have been exercised on the course of the Napoleonic wars by three Chassidic leaders, whether as supporters or opponents of Napoleon—Jacob Yizhak from Lublin, Israel of Kosnitz,

and Menachem Mendel of Rymanov. All three died within a single year (1814–1815)—the year of Napoleon's downfall.

[20] For the Enlightenment movement see Joseph Meisl's " Haskalah " (1919).

[21] The two principal Yiddish dramas of Anski, both drawn from Chassidic life, are " Zwischen zwei Welten ", or " Der Dibbuk ", and the fragmentary " Tog und Nacht ". The former has become very well known through the performances of the Vilna dramatic company and of the " Habimah " (in Bialik's Hebrew translation). Among the best modern depicters of Chassidism are Sholem Ash in his story " Der Tillimsoger " (*v*. p. 26), and S. J. Agnon, who has reproduced with great fidelity the mode of life and feeling of the Chassidim, down to their very language.

IX

CABBALISTIC TENDENCIES OUTSIDE OF JUDAISM

If we compare the history of Jewish mysticism with that of the numerous mystical movements in Christian Europe,[1] we cannot fail to notice instances of what may be called an invisible contact between the two—that is to say of the same tendencies at work in both in certain countries at certain times. Thus it can hardly be an accident that the essentially pietistic movement of German Jewish Chassidism fell in the age of the pious monks and nuns in Germany, or that the Cabbalah flourished in Provence almost at the same time as the Provençal mysticism of the Catharians.[2] Similarly the Spanish Cabbalah was contemporaneous with the Spanish-Christian mysticism, while the earliest dissemination of the Zohar coincided with the lifetime of the greatest German mystic, Meister Eckhardt (1260–1329).

In addition to this unseen contact there were also direct contacts which became more marked as time went on. The earliest Christian scholar who is known to have occupied himself with the Cabbalah[3] is the Catalonian Raymundus Lullus (1235–1315), who is said to have regarded the Cabbalah as the gate of all knowledge, and who wrote a book "De auditu Cabbalistico" in which the Cabbalah is described as "the absorption of every precious divinely revealed truth by the rational soul of man". How far his "Ars Magna", i.e., the art of acquiring knowledge through the manipulation of letters of the alphabet, was influenced by the Cabbalistic use of letters, is a question that still requires investigation.[4]

A quickened interest in the Cabbalah accompanied the new Hebraic humanism which was produced by the Renaissance. Almost at the same time Johannes Reuchlin composed two Cabbalistic works in Latin, "De Arte Cabbalistica" and "De Verbo Mirifico", and Pico de

Mirandola published in Rome a number of Cabbalistic theses under the title of " Conclusiones Cabbalisticæ ".

These early attempts to create a " Christian Cabbalah " sprang from various motives. One was an attempt to convert the Jews by pointing out real or fancied agreements between the Cabbalah and the Christian dogma. Another, which is observable in many thinkers of that time, including to some extent the philosopher Giordano Bruno, is a leaning to magic and occultism. A third is a tendency to discover in the Cabbalah, as also in the mystical traditions of antiquity (Pythagoreans, Egyptians, etc.) the source of all deeper knowledge. Thus, for example, Reuchlin tries hard to derive the Christian dogma of the Trinity from the Cabbalah,[5] and in so doing goes deeply into the mystical significance of the sounds of the Hebrew divine name (the Tetragrammaton), from which he makes the name of Jesus originate by the addition of the S sound. He also sees in the Cabbalah the origin of Pythagoreanism.[6]

To the second class belong above all the works of Agrippa of Nettesheim and Athanasius Kircher. The former in his comprehensive work " De occulta philosophia " occupies himself largely with number-magic, making much use of the so-called " magic squares ", which were known also to Jewish thinkers (e.g. Abraham ibn Ezra) and were often used as amulets.[7] Kircher finds in the Cabbalah the origin of the ancient mysteries which were brought by Abraham to Egypt.

The Hebrew language as such was assiduously studied in these circles, as is testified by the numerous Latin translations of Hebrew works. These included also Cabbalistic works, such as the Sefer Yezirah by Postel and Rittangel and a number of Cabbalistic writings (including the three oldest passages from the Zohar v. p. 88) contained in the " Cabbalah Denudata " by Knorr von Rosenroth, which appeared in 1677. Hebrew, however, was also used as a holy, or we might say magical, language. And even the Hebrew grammarians, in particular the two Helmonts (father and son), display traces of a belief in the mystical character of this language.

In the succeeding period we meet, especially in Germany and England, isolated Cabbalistic doctrines and expressions in writers connected with Rosicurcianism and Freemasonry, whom we find for instance quoting Hebrew name-symbols and terms of the Sefiroth doctrine, which they develop further after their own manner. We also, however, come across independent systems of thought which are akin to the Cabbalistic wisdom, but regarding which we cannot always determine whether the resemblance is due to conscious borrowing or to thinking on parallel lines. Waite in his book " The Holy Cabbalah " mentions a whole series of English Christian Cabbalists of the 17th and 18th centuries, who stood in close contact with Rosicrucianism or similar movements, among them the well known alchemist[s] Robert Fludd, the celebrated representative of Cambridge Platonism, Henry More, who wrote about the Merkabah as he understood it, Thomas Vaughan, Cudworth, and Thomas Burnet.

Cabbalistic leanings took a peculiar turn in the second half of the eighteenth century in France, where Martines de Pascally erected a Cabbalistic system on Catholic lines, and where, just before the Revolution, the celebrated Louis Claude de Saint Martin founded under the influence of Cabbalistic ideas the modern Occultism, which his successors developed into something closely approaching modern theosophy and anthroposophy. Among the most important of these successors are Fabre d'Olivet, who reintroduced the occult method of studying the Hebrew language ; Stanislaus de Guaita, Eliphaz Levi (pseudonym of Abbé Louis Constant), who professed to see the foundation of all wisdom in a Cabbalah of a very mystical and subjective kind, and himself composed a " Livre de Splendeur " ; the occultist historian St. Yves d'Alveydre, whose principal work is entitled, after its main subject, " Mission de Juifs " ; Papus (d'Encausse), author of a work on Cabbalah ; and finally Edouard Schuré, author of " The Great Initiates ".

Naturally there is no end to the mystical and philosophical systems which while quite independent of the Cabbalah yet show close resemblances to it. Attention may be drawn here to three such systems, one of which presents striking parallels to the Cabbalah, though we have no evidence of its being actually derived from it, while the other two emanated from Jews, but exercised their strongest influence outside of Judaism.

Jacob Böhme, the "shoemaker of Görlitz" (1545–1624), in his profound but obscure reflections, rendered still more obscure by the difficulty of his German style, speaks of an "Ungrund" (un-ground) of the world, which he also designates the "First Will" and the "Eternal Nothing", expressions which at once remind us of the "Ayin" (v. p. 96) and the Primordial Will (v. pp. 74, 75) of the Cabbalah. Of this "un-ground" it is further said by him that it resembles a hidden fire, which " exists and does not exist "— a characteristic expression of the Zohar. Other parallels are to be found in the distinction drawn between a " dark " world or world of fire and a world of light[9] which springs from it, in the personal, subjective sense attached to the terms "heaven" and "hell", in the opposition between the cosmic principles of "Wrath" or "Fire of Wrath" and "Love", in the doctrine of the "labelling of things", which thus are only indications of the reality which expresses itself in them, and in the mystical treatment of the sounds of German words.

In his "Dialoghi di Amore" Judah Abravanel[10] develops a "philosophy of love" based on the Symposium of Plato, which was a favourite work with the Platonists of the Renaissance period. Love is for him the bond of union between all beings and all stages of existence in the universe. Heinz Pflaum sums up his teaching in its historical relationships as follows : " His picture of the universe takes from scholasticism the hierarchic structure of the emanation doctrine, from contemporary thought the idea of animation by the universal principle of love, from Judaism the speculative elements (the doctrine of the attributes, and of the creation and the eschatology), and from Plato the interpretation (the doctrine of Ideas). The mystical goal of existence is the linking together of the whole universe and also of the individual soul with God, without detriment to the transcendence of God. Perceiving in himself the first beauty, God embraces the world in an affectionate knowledge, and man attains to a loving knowledge of God in so far as he discerns the true form of the beautiful."

In a broader sense the philosophy of Baruch Spinoza can also be regarded as an offshoot of Jewish mysticism. While obviously its sources are to be sought for the most part outside of Judaism—in the contemporary Cartesian philosophy, in the piety of the Protestant sects then flourishing in Holland, and even in the Stoicism of antiquity— yet the Jewish element in this system can by no means be denied.[10] Spinoza may actually have been influenced by Moses Maimonides, Moses Cordoveiro, Abraham Hereira, and, as Gebhardt has shown, by Leo Hebræus.[11] But the important thing is that his mind works on Jewish lines.[12] The bold attempt of the " Ethics " to derive by a logical process both the world of nature and of man equally from God ; the contrast drawn between the bondage of man in the natural condition and his growing freedom through the approach to God ; the placing of the starting-point of all becoming in the eternity of the divine substance and, on the other side, of its culmination in the free love of God—all this can properly be regarded as Jewish metaphysic and ethic. And all this rests on the mystical postulate in the thinking man of the " third kind of knowledge ", that is, the immediately intuitive insight into being or into the " ideas " of things, culminating in that " intellectual love of God " (amor Dei intellectualis), which again (according to the 36th statement of the fifth portion of the " Ethics ") is nothing else than " the love with which God loves Himself ".

In more recent times many echoes of Cabbalistic thought are again to be found in Germany, in the classical literature and philosophy. The chief representatives of this tendency are J. G. Haman (the " Magician of the North "), the friend of Herder, the " theosophist " Franz von Baader, and above all the philosopher Wilhelm Friedrich Schelling.[13] In Schelling's work " Die Gottheiten von Samothrake ", which contains also many mystical combinations of Hebrew roots, we find the following remark : " The Quabbalah contains ruins and fragments, if you will much distorted, but nevertheless remnants of that primitive system which is the key to all religious systems." In his period efforts were frequently made, especially in Germany, to find a philosophic basis for the Cabbalah, e.g. by Fr. Kleuker and Franz Joseph Molitor, who in his work " Philosophische Geschichte der jüdischen Tradition " expresses himself as follows regarding the study of the Cabbalah : " . . . It seems therefore to be urgently necessary that the investigation into the old tradition of Judaism should be taken up at the point where it was broken off in the 17th century, so as to achieve the end that was once aimed at by Mirandola, Galatinus, Reuchlin, Knorr, Vitringa, and others, but for which their time was not yet ripe. Such a research, conducted with superior insight, into the mysteries of the ancient people of Israel . . . will in our opinion be well calculated to awaken Christian mysticism at its source . . . to base the structure of theology on its deepest theosophical principles, and in this way to prepare a common ground for an eventual reunion of the sundered religious groups. Such research will in particular . . . pave the way to a true history of the origins of man, and serve as the one true guide to the dark labyrinth of the myths, mysteries, and social systems of the various peoples, and in this way help to give precision to our vague ideas of that which was and which will be, and to place in a clearer light much which is now only surmise."

Among modern occultist movements theosophy, with its Indian leanings, has paid little attention to Jewish mysticism, save for its founder Madame P. H. Blavatsky, who in her well known work " Secret Doctrine ", and still more in her " Isis Unveiled ", has taken from the Zohar and the Cabbalah. To a much greater extent the Anthroposophy founded by Rudolf Steiner has in many circles again turned attention to the hidden meaning of the biblical account of the creation, to the occult element in the Hebrew language and in language in general (Herman Beckh, Arnold Wadler), to the historical relations of the Jewish Gnosis with early Christianity, to the connection of Rosicrucianism with the old mystical movements, and to efforts to place the whole of knowledge on a new basis.

Notes to Chapter IX

[1] With regard to the connection of Jewish mysticism with Islam, it may be noted that Grætz traces back the concepts of the " Shiur Komah " (*v.* p. 56) to anthropomorphic tendencies in Mohammedan mysticism, while Zunz would assign the origin of the Cabbalah altogether to such influences. Ariel Benzion finds points of contact between the Zohar mysticism and the contemporaneous Islamic mysticism in Spain.

[2] A medieval sect with very ascetic tendencies. *V.* Encyclopedia Britannica, *s.v.*

[3] Such relations are referred to by Tennemann in the 8th volume of his " History of Philosophy ", and had in fact already been mentioned in the 15th century by Nicolaus Cusanus. *V.* also Adolf Frank in the introduction to his book on the Cabbalah.

[4] A contemporary of Raymundus Lullus, Arnold of Villanova, made great use of Latin letter-mysticism after the Cabbalistic model for his Christian-messianic calculations. (Communicated by Dr. Beate Hirsch-Reich of Oxford.)

[5] E.g., he deduces the Trinity of Father, Son and Holy Ghost from a notarikon on the word ברא in the first verse of Genesis : ב = בֵּן, ר = רוח, and א = אב.

[6] Both Reuchlin and Pico had Jewish teachers—the former Yehiel Loans, the latter the baptised John (Peter) Alemanus.

[7] Whether the amulets discovered by Ahrens containing figures of Greek gods are Jewish or only Hebrew is a question.

[8] Although the alchemists frequently appeal to the Cabbalah, and even created an "alchemistic Cabbalah ", very few traces of alchemy properly so called are to be found in the Cabbalistic literature. The only Cabbalistic work of this character is " The Purifying Fire " (*Esh Metzaref*), the cabbalistic parts of which according to Sholem date from about the 16th century. It has been published by Wynn Westcott in an English translation.

[9] The lofty function of light (*cf.* pp. 29, 94) is expressed in the following passage of the " Six Theosophic Points " : " God's kingdom is found only in the bright clear light of freedom, in love and gentleness : for that is the property of the white clear light."

[10] Judah Abravanel, the eldest son of Isaac Abravanel (*v.* pp. 132, 136), was born in Lisbon about 1460. On the expulsion of the Jews from Spain he fled to Genoa, and then to Venice, where he died in 1535. In Spain he had been physician to an Admiral. He subsequently devoted

much study to the neo-Platonist philosophy, and was in close touch with Pico de Mirandola. His principal work, " Dialoghi di Amore ", was composed in Italian. By his Christian contemporaries he was known as " Leone Ebreo " (Leo Hebræus).

[11] For Spinoza's relation to Jewish religious philosophy see especially Joel's " Beiträge zur Geschichte der Philosophie " and J. Freudenthal, " Das Leben Spinoza's " ; his relations to the Cabbalah have been dealt with by S. Gelbhaus, Isaac Misses, H. Sonne, and others. On the anti-Jewish side Spinoza and the Cabbalah were from the very first, as for instance in the notorious work of Wachter, identified in the most peculiar manner, on the ground, for instance, that both of them deified external nature.

[12] This applies especially to the so-called " Small Tractate "—on God, on Man, and on Man's Happiness—written in Dutch and first discovered in the 19th century. Of all the writings of Spinoza this is the most religious-mystical in character. The knowledge of God, for instance, is here still designated a revelation of God. The idea of the " amor Dei intellectualis " is derived directly from the third part of the " Dialoghi di Amore ".

[13] Numerous points of contact with the cabbalistic mysticism can be found in the " Philosophie der Mythologie " and also in the " Philosophie der Offenbarung ". Hegel comes close to the Cabbalah in his trinitarian scheme of Thesis, Antithesis, and Synthesis, also in positing " Not-being " as the basis from which springs " being ", " existence " being the product of both (v. p. 118).

APPENDIX

I

THE WISDOM OF SOLOMON
VII, 22²—VIII⁹

(Translation by W. O. E. OESTERLEY)

For there is in her a spirit of understanding, holy,
Sole-born, manifold, subtil,
Mobil, lucid, unpolluted,
Clear, inviolable, loving goodness, keen,
Unhindered, beneficent, loving toward man . . .

For she is a vapour of the power of God,
And a clear effluence of the glory of the Almighty ;
Therefore nothing defiled findeth entrance into her.
For she is a reflection from everlasting light,
And an unspotted mirror of the working of God,
And the image of his goodness.
Though being (but) one she can do all things,
And (though) abiding within herself she reneweth all things,
And from generation to generation passing into holy souls,
She maketh men friends of God and prophets.
For nothing doth God love save him that dwelleth with Wisdom.
For she is more beautiful than the sun,
And above every constellation of the stars (in beauty),
Being compared with light she is found superior . . .
For night followeth this,
Whereas evil prevaileth not over Wisdom,
But reacheth from end to end (of the earth) mightily,
And ordered all things fitly.

Her I loved and sought diligently from my youth,
Yea, I sought (her) to lead her home as my bride,
And I became enamoured of her beauty . . .
For she teacheth self-control and prudence,
Righteousness and manliness,
Than which nothing in life is more profitable for men.
And if a man longeth also for much experience,
She knoweth the things of old, and divineth the things to come ;
She understandeth subtilties of arguments and the interpreta-
    tions of dark sayings ;

Signs and wonders doth she foresee,
And the issues of seasons and times.
I determined therefore to take her unto me to live with me,
Knowing that she will be to me a counsellor of what is good,
And a comfort in cares and grief.

II.

FROM THE WORKS OF PHILO.

And his exordium . . . is most admirable; embracing the creation of the world under the idea that the law corresponds to the world and the world to the law, and that a man who is obedient to the law, being, by so doing, a citizen of the world, arranges his actions with reference to the intention of nature, in harmony with which the whole world is regulated.

(*On the Creation of the World*, I, 1.)

And after he has conducted him [*sc.* Abraham] out, he says to him : Look up to heaven and count the stars if thou art able to number them ; thus shall be thy seed (Gen. XV, 5). . . . 'Thus shall thy seed be,' says God, as the ethereal firmament which thou beholdest, so heavenly, so full of unshadowed and pure brilliancy as most thoroughly like the stars, beautifully adorned, having an arrangement which knows no deviation, but which is always the same and proceeding in the same way. For he means him to speak of the soul of the wise man as a copy of heaven, or, if one may use such a hyperbolic expression, as an actual heaven upon earth, having pure appearances in the air, and well arranged motions, and harmonious progress, and periodical revolutions of divine character, star-like and brilliant rays of virtue.

(*On Who is the Heir of Divine Things*, XVII.

Translation of C. D. Yonge.)

We came to sojourn (Gen. XLVII, 4) not to settle there . . . for in reality a wise man's soul ever finds heaven to be his fatherland and earth a foreign country and regards as his own the dwelling-place of wisdom and that of the body as outlandish ; and looks on himself as a stranger and sojourner in it. Accordingly, when Mind, the ruler of the flock, taking the flock of the soul in hand with the law of Nature as his instructor shews it the way with vigorous leadership, he renders it well worthy of praise and approval, even as he subjects it to blame if he disregard Nature's law and behave slackly and carelessly.

With good reason then will the one take to him the name of a king and be hailed shepherd . . . but the other . . . entitled caitiff . . .

(*On Husbandry*, 65.)

' . . And he dreamed a dream. And behold a ladder was planted firmly on the ground the head of which reached the heaven and the angels of God were ascending and descending along it ' (Gen. XXVIII, 12). By the ladder in this thing which is called the world is figuratively understood the air, the foundation of which is the earth and the head is the heaven. . . .

Is it not then absurd that that element by means of which the other elements have been filled with vitality, should itself be destitute of living things ? Therefore let no one deprive the most excellent nature of living creatures of the most excellent of those elements which surround the earth ; that is to say : of the air. For not only is it not alone deserted by all things besides, but rather, like a populous city, it is full of imperishable and immortal citizens, souls equal in numbers to the stars.

Now of these souls some descend upon the earth with a view to being bound up in mortal bodies, those namely which are most nearly connected with the earth, and which are lovers of the body. But some soar upwards, being again distinguished according to the definitions and time which have been appointed by nature. Of these those which are influenced by a desire for mortal life and which have been familiarised to it again return to it. But others, condemning the body of great folly and trifling, have pronounced it a prison and a grave, and flying from it as from a house of correction or a tomb, have raised themselves aloft on light wings towards the ether, and have devoted their whole lives to sublime speculations.

There are others, again, the purest and most excellent of all, which have received greater and more divine intellects, never by any chance desiring any earthly thing whatever, but being as it were lieutenants of the Ruler of the universe as though they were the eyes and ears of the great king, beholding and listening to everything.

(*On Dreams* II, xxii. Translation of
C. D. Yonge.)

III

1. MERKABAH MYSTIC

From the Hebrew Book of Enoch, The Host of Heaven, ch. 18.[1]

Rabbi Ishmael said : Metatron, the Angel, the Prince of the Presence,[2] the glory of all heaven, said to me :
" The Angels of the First Heaven, whenever they see their prince, they dismount from their horses and fall on their faces.

And the Prince of the First Heaven, when he sees the Prince of the Second Heaven, he dismounts, removes the crown of glory from his head, and falls on his face."

This continues through all the seven heavens. Then follow the seventy-two Princes of the Kingdoms, then the Doorkeepers of the successive Halls (Hechaloth),[3] *then the four Great Princes (the Archangels), then numerous angels with various, often phantastic names. All are introduced with the same form of expression, some angels, however, being described more particularly, e.g. :*

" Zarzakiel the Prince, who is appointed to write down the merits of Israel on the Throne of Glory.

Anaphiel the prince who keeps the keys of the heavenly halls," etc.

Then :

" Why is he called Sopheriel, the Lifegiver ? Because he is appointed over the books of the living (of life), so that every one whom the Holy One, blessed be He, will bring into life, he writes in the book of the living (of life), by authority of MAQOM.[4]

Thou mightest perhaps say, since the Holy One, blessed be He, is sitting on a throne, they also are sitting when writing ? (Answer) The Scripture teaches us (1 Kings, XXII, 19, 2 Chron. XVIII, 18) ; ' And all the hosts of heaven are standing by Him '. ' The host of heaven,' it is said, in order to show us that even the Great Princes, none like whom there is in the high heavens, do not fulfil the requests of the Shekinah otherwise than standing.

But how is it possible that they are able to write when they are standing ?

It is like this :

One is standing on the wheel of the tempest, and the other is standing on the wheel of the storm-wind.

[1] English translation taken from Odeberg, " The Book of Enoch ".
[2] Sar Ha-Panim, i.e., Michael, *v. p.* 52.
[3] The Hechaloth are the compartments of the seventh heaven, *v. p.* 51.
[4] A name of God, *v. p.* 19 and p. 171.

The one is clad in kingly garments, the other is clad in kingly garments.

The one is wrapped in a mantle of majesty, the other is wrapped in a mantle of majesty.

The one is crowned with a royal crown and the other is crowned with a royal crown.

The one's body is full of eyes[1] and the other's body is full of eyes.

The appearance of one is like unto the appearance of lightnings and the appearance of the other is like unto the appearance of lightnings.

The eyes of the one are like the sun in its might and the eyes of the other are like the sun in its might."

The description of the outer appearance of the angels is continued through their various limbs (wings, lips, tongue, mouth, etc.), with indication of their gigantic proportions.[2] *Then:*

" From the one's tongue a torch is burning, and from the tongue of the other a torch is burning.

On the head of the one there is a sapphire stone, and on the head of the other there is a sapphire stone.

On the shoulders of the one there is a wheel of a swift cherub, and on the shoulders of the other there is a wheel of a swift cherub.

One has in his hand a burning scroll, the other has in his hand a burning scroll.

One has in his hand a flaming style, the other has in his hand a flaming style.

The length of the scroll is 3,000 myriads of parasangs; the size of the style is 3,000 myriads of parasangs; the size of every letter that they write is 365 parasangs . . ."

2. THE HEAVENLY KEDUSHAH
From the Hebrew Book of Enoch, ch. 35.[3]

After a description of the angels who stand before the Throne of the Divine Majesty, the *Kisse ha-Kabod*,[4] it goes on:

" And in the hour when the time draws nigh to say the Holy (then) first there goes forth a whirlwind from before the Holy One, blessed be He, and bursts upon the camp of Shekina, and

[1] V. Ezekiel, I, 18.

[2] *V. p.* 56

[3] Translation by Odeberg.

[4] *Kabod* is the form in which the Deity appears, not the Deity itself, *v. p.* 19.

there arises a great commotion among them, as it is written (Jer. XXX, 23) ' Behold the whirlwind of the Lord goeth forth with fury, a continuing commotion '. At that moment thousand thousands of them are changed into sparks, thousand thousands of them into firebrands, thousand thousands into flashes, thousand thousands into males, thousand thousands into females, thousand thousands of them into winds, thousand thousands into burning fires, thousand thousands into flames, thousand thousands into chashmals[1] of light; until they take upon themselves the yoke of the Kingdom of Heaven,[2] the high and lifted-up, of the Creator of them all, with fear, dread, awe and trembling, with commotion, anguish, terror and trepidation. Then they are changed again into their former shape to have the fear of their King before them always, as they have set their hearts on saying the Song continually, as it is written (Is. VI, 3): ' And one cried unto another and said, (Holy, Holy, Holy) '."

THE KEDUSHAH IN HEAVEN AND ON EARTH
(From the Pirke Hechaloth).

Said Rabbi Ishmael: " Hail Israel, how are they beloved of the Holy One, praised be He, more than the ministering angels! For in the hour when these desire to sing the hymn of praise on high, there come round about the Throne of Glory streams of fire and mountains of flame, and the Holy One, praised be He, says: ' Sit ye and be silent, every angel, every *Chayah*, every *Ophan*, every Seraph, whom I have created, until I first hear the voice of the songs and praises of Israel, My children. And when the time comes for chanting the hymn of praise, then stands Shema'el, the mighty prince, the greatly honoured and revered, at the window of the lower heaven listening for the voice of songs and praises which ascend from the earth from the synagogues and houses of study, in order to summon the denizens of Araboth to hear them. Why does he do so ? Because it is not permitted to the ministering angels to utter the hymn of praise before Israel have commenced it. For so it says: ' Exalt ye the Lord our God and worship at His holy mountain ' (Ps. XCIX, 9). These are the ministering angels and all the angels of the firmament, when they hear the songs and praises which are uttered below; for then they also commence the chant above with the

---

[1] See Ezek, I, 4, 27, and p. 45.
[2] A regular expression for the acceptance of God's sovereignty.

threefold 'Holy'. And why is he called Shema'el? Because he stands at every gate and tries to hear (*shema'*) the voice of the songs and praises which ascend from the synagogues and houses of study to each one of the firmaments. In this hour the Holy One, praised be He, sits on the throne of His majesty, and His majesty fills the whole earth, as it says: ' The whole earth is full of His glory ' (Is. VI, 3). All those ministering angels also have each his particular task, because the Merkabah is spread in front of them and the Shekinah is over them and streams of fire go to and fro between them."

IV

FROM TALMUD BABLI AND MIDRASH

PRE-EXISTENCE

Seven things were created before the world was created and these are they : The Torah, Repentance, the Garden of Eden, Gehenna, the Throne of Glory, the Temple and the Name of the Messiah.

(Pesachim, 54a.)

THE FIRST MAN.

It has been taught, R. Meir used to say : The dust of the first man was gathered from all parts of the earth, for it is written : Thine eyes did see mine unformed substance (Ps. CXXXIX, 16), and further it is written : The eyes of the Lord run to and fro through the whole earth (Zech. IV, 10). R. Oshaia said in Rab's name : Adam's trunk came from Babylon, his head from Erez Israel, the most exalted, his limbs from other lands and his private parts, according to R. Acha, from Akis de Agma[1].

(Sanhedrin 38a—b.)

TRACES OF SEFIROTH TEACHINGS.

Seven Middoth[2] serve before the Throne of Glory : Wisdom, Right and Justice, Love and Mercy, Truth and Peace.

(Abot de R. Nathan, chap. 37.)

[1] A town, near Pumbedita, notorious on account of the loose morals of its inhabitants.

[2] Personifications of the Divine Attributes.

Ten are the qualities with which the world has been created: Wisdom, Insight, Knowledge, Force, Appeal,[1] Power, Justice, Right, Love and Compassion.

(Hagiga, 12b.)

THE PRIMORDIAL LIGHT.

. . . R. Eleazar said : The light which the Holy One, blessed be He, created on the first day, Adam could see thereby from one end of the world to the other ; but as soon as the Holy One beheld the generation of the Flood and the generation of Dispersion (Gen. XI, 9) and saw that their actions were corrupt He arose and hid it from them, for it is said : But from the wicked their light is withholden (Job XXXVIII, 15). And for whom did He reserve it ? For the righteous in the time to come[2], for it is said: And God saw the light that it was good (Gen. I, 4) and good means only the righteous, for it is said : Say ye of the righteous that he is good (Is. III, 10). As soon as He saw the light that He had reserved for the righteous, He rejoiced at the light of the righteous.

(Hagiga, 12a.)

THE MESSIAH.

It is taught, R. Yose says : Alas for people that they see but know not what they see ; they stay but know not on what they stand.[3] What does the earth rest on ? On the pillars, for it is said : . . . the pillars upon the waters, the waters upon the mountains . . . the mountains on the wind, the wind upon the storm.[4] Storm is suspended on the arm of the Holy One, blessed be He, for it is said : And underneath are the everlasting arms (Deut. XXXIII, 27). But the Sages say : [The world] rests on twelve pillars, for it is said : He set the borders to the peoples according to the number [of the tribes] of the children of Israel (Deut. XXXII, 8). And some say : Seven pillars, for it is said : She hath hewn out her seven pillars (Prov. IX, 1). R. Eleazar-ben Shamua says: [It rests] on one pillar and its name is Righteous, for it is said : But Righteous (Zaddik) is the foundation of the world (Prov. X, 25).

(Hagiga, 12b.)

---

[1] Literally, repelling force.
[2] i.e., the Messianic era, *v.* Abot II, 16.
[3] This phrase is repeatedly used in the Zohar, e.g. I, 83 a–l.
[4] These statements are taken from several places of the Bible.

At the beginning of the creation of the world was born the King Messiah, who mounted into God's thoughts before the world was made.

(Pesikta Rabbati, 33.)

THE SHEKINAH.

. . . When Adam sinned the Shekinah ascended to the first firmament. When Cain sinned it ascended to the second firmament. When Enosh sinned it ascended to the third firmament. When the generation of the Flood sinned it ascended to the fourth firmament. When the generation of the Tower sinned it ascended to the fifth firmament. When the men of Sodom sinned it ascended to the sixth firmament. When the Egyptians sinned in the days of Abraham it ascended to the seventh firmament. Correspondingly seven righteous men arose who brought it down again to the earth. Abraham by his virtues brought it down from the seventh to the sixth firmament. Isaac arose and brought it down from the sixth to the fifth. Jacob arose and brought it down from the fifth to the fourth. Levi arose and brought it down from the fourth to the third. Kehath arose and brought it down from the third to the second. Amram arose and brought it down from the second to the first. Then Moses arose and brought it down to earth. . . .

Midrash Rabbah, *The Song of Songs,* V, 1.

. . . The Rabbis made a comparison with a king who gave his daughter in marriage to someone in another country. The people of this country said to him : Your majesty, it accords with your honour and it is only right that your daughter should be in the same country with you. He said to them : What does it matter to you ? They replied : Perhaps later you will visit her and stay with her on account of your love for her. He then replied : I will give my daughter in marriage out of the country, but I will reside with you in this town. So when the Holy One, blessed be He, announced his intention of giving the Torah to Israel, the ministering angels said to the Holy One, blessed be He : Sovereign of the Universe, Thou art He whose (asher) majesty is over the heaven ; it is Thy happiness (ishureka), Thy glory, and Thy praise that the Torah should be in the heaven. He said to them : What does it matter to you ? They said : Perhaps to-morrow Thou wilt cause Thy Divine Presence to abide in the lower world. Then the Holy One, blessed be He, replied to them : I will give My Torah to the dwellers on earth but I will abide with the celestial beings.

I will give away my daughter with her marriage portion to another country in order that she may pride herself with her husband on her beauty and charm and be honoured as befits a king's daughter. But I will abide with you in the upper world. . . .

Ibid. VIII, 11.

It has been taught: Rabbi Shimeon ben Yochai said: Come and see how beloved are Israel in the sight of God, in that to every place to which they were exiled the Shekinah went with them. (Examples follow of Egypt, Babylon.) . . . And when they will be redeemed in the future, the Shekinah will be with them, as it says: ' Then the Lord thy God will return [with] thy captivity ' (Deut. XXX, 3). . . . The fathers of Samuel and Levi were sitting in the synagogue which moved and settled in Nehardea. The Shekinah came and they heard a sound of tumult and rose and went out. . . .

(Megillah, 29a.)

THE HOLY NAME.

Our Rabbis taught : Ten times did the high priest pronounce the [Ineffable] Name on that day (*sc.* the Day of Atonement): three times at the first confession, thrice at the second confession, thrice in connection with the he-goat to be sent away and once in connection with the lots. And there have been times that when he pronounced the Name his voice was heard even unto Jericho.

(Yoma, 39b.)

And when the Priests and the People standing in the Temple Court heard the fully-pronounced Name come forth from the mouth of the High Priest, they bent their knees, bowed down, fell on their faces and called out : Blessed be the Name of His glorious kingdom for ever and ever.[1]

(Yoma, 69b.)

OTHER NAMES OF GOD.

Since the Sanctuary was destroyed it is enough for the world to use only two letters [of the Tetragrammaton].[2]

(Erubin, 18b.)

---

[1] The whole passage is included in the Kippur liturgy.
[2] Viz. the J and the H forming the name JH.

And he lighted (wajifga) upon the place (Gen. XXVIII, 11). R. Huna said in R. Ami's name : Why do we give a changed name to the Holy One, blessed be He, and call him the ' Place ' ? Because he is the place of the world. R. Jose bar Halafta said : We do not know whether God is the place of His world or whether His world is His place, but from the verse : Behold there is a place with me (Ex. XXXIII, 21) it follows that the Lord is the place of His world but His world is not His place.

(*Midrash Bereshit Rabbah* II, 99.)

THE REVELATION.

R. Simeon ben Lakish said : The scroll which God gave to Moses was of white fire and its writing of black fire. It was itself fire and it was hewn out of fire and completely formed of fire and given in fire, as it says : At His right hand was a fiery law unto them (Deut. XXXIII, 2).

(Midrash Rabbah, *Song of Songs*, V, 11.)

ANGELS.

R. Yochanan said : The righteous are greater than the ministering angels. For it is said : He answered : Lo, I see four men loose, walking in the midst of the fire and they have no hurt, and the form of the fourth is like the Son of God.

R. Simeon said : There is not a single herb but has a constellation in heaven which strikes it and says 'Grow', as it is written : Knowest thou the ordinances of the heavens ? Canst thou establish the dominion thereof in the earth ? (Job XXXVIII, 33).

(*Sanhedrin*, 93a.)

THE SATAN.

. . . They ordered a fast of three days and three nights whereupon he was surrendered to them. . . . Thereupon the prophet said to Israel: This is the evil desire of idolatry. . . . Thereupon they said : How shall we act ? Perhaps, God forbid, they might have mercy upon him from heaven. . . . The prophet said unto them : Cast him in a leaden pot, closing its opening with lead. . . . They said : Since this is a time of grace let us pray for mercy for the Tempter to evil. They prayed for mercy and he was handed over to them. He said to them : Realise that if you kill him, the world goes down. They imprisoned him for three days, then locked in the whole land of Israel and could not find it. Thereupon they said : What shall we do now ? Shall we kill him ? The world would then go down. Shall we beg for half mercy ? They do not grant 'halves' in heaven.—They put out his eyes and let him go.

(*Yoma*, 69*b*.)

ISRAEL.

R. Abun said : This lily when the sun beats upon it withers, but when the dew falls it revives. So Israel, so long as the shadow of Esau is in the ascendant, seem to be withered in this world, but when the shadow of Esau will pass away, Israel shall blossom forth, as it says : I will be as the dew unto Israel, he shall blossom as the lily (Hos. XIV, 6). Just as the lily expires only with its scent, so Israel expires only with religious acts and good deeds. Just as the whole purpose of the lily is to give scent, so the righteous are created only for the deliverance of Israel. Just as the lily is set on the table of kings at the beginning and at the end of the meal, so Israel are found in this world and are found in the next world. So as the lily is conspicuous among plants so Israel are conspicuous among the nations, as it says : All that see them shall acknowledge them (Is. LXI, 9). Just as the lily is kept for Sabbaths and festivals so Israel are kept for the deliverance of to-morrow.

(Midrash Rabbah. *Song of Songs* II, 2, 6.)

Thine eyes are [as] doves ; like doves : that is : thy quality is like that of the dove. Just as the dove brought light into the world so Israel bring light into the world, as it says : ' And nations shall walk at thy light ' (Is. LX, 3.) . . .

(*Ibid.* IV, 2.)

' I sleep, but my heart waketh.' Said the Community of Israel before the Holy One, blessed be He : ' Sovereign of the Universe ! I am asleep in the neglect of religious observance, but my heart is awake for the performance of charity. I am asleep in respect of righteous deeds, but my heart is awake [in the desire] to do them. I am asleep in respect of the sacrifices, but my heart is awake for the recital of ' Shema ' and Prayer. I am asleep in respect of the Temple, but my heart is awake for synagogues and houses of study. I am asleep in respect of the end [*sc.* of the end's time], but my heart is awake for the redemption. I am asleep in respect of the redemption, but the heart of the Holy One, blessed be He, is awake to redeem me. R. Hiyya-bar Abba said: Where do we find that God is called the heart of Israel? In the following verse: God is the rock, my heart, and my portion for ever' (Ps. LXXIII, 26).

(*Ibid.* V, 2.)

RESURRECTION.

Mishnah: All Israel have a portion in the world to come, for it is written: 'Thy people are all righteous, they shall inherit the land for ever, the branch of my planting, the work of my hands that I may be glorified. But the following have no portion therein: he who maintains that resurrection is not a biblical doctrine, the Torah was not divinely revealed, and an Epikoros[1] . . .

Gemara: And why such [severity]? A Tanna taught: Since he denied the resurrection of the dead therefore he shall not share in that resurrection, for in all the measures [of punishment or reward] taken by the Holy One, blessed be He, the Divine act befits the [human] dead.

(*Sanhedrin*, 90a—90b.)

A sectarian [min] said to Gebiha ben Pesisa, 'Woe to you, ye wicked, who maintain that the dead will revive; if even the living die, shall the dead live!' He replied: 'Woe to you, ye wicked, who maintain that the dead will not revive; if what was not [now] lives, surely what was lived will live again!'

The School of R. Ismael taught: It can be deduced from glassware: if glassware, which, though made by the breath of human beings, can yet be repaired when broken; then how much more so man, created by the breath of the Holy One, blessed be He.

(*Sanhedrin*, 91a.)

BODY AND SOUL IN THE SIN OF MAN.

Antoninus said to Rabbi: 'The body and the soul can both free themselves from judgement. Thus the body can plead: The soul has sinned, [the proof being] that from the day it left me I lie like a dumb stone in the grave [powerless to do aught]. Whilst the soul can say: The body has sinned, [the proof being] that from the day I departed from it I fly about in the air like

---

[1] An Epicurean, i.e. a lascivious person.

a bird [and commit no sin].' He replied : 'I will tell thee a parable. To what may this be compared ? To a human king who owned a beautiful orchard which contained splendid figs. Now, he appointed two watchmen therein, one lame and the other blind. [One day] the lame man said to the blind. 'I see beautiful figs in the orchard. Come and take me upon thy shoulder, that we may procure and eat them.' So the lame bestrode the blind, procured and ate them. Some time after, the owner of the orchard came and inquired of them 'Where are those beautiful figs ? ' The lame man replied : 'Have I then feet to walk with ? ' The blind man replied : 'Have I then eyes to see with ? ' What did he do ? He placed the lame upon the blind and judged them together. So will the Holy One, blessed be He, bring the soul, [re]place it in the body, and judge them together. . . .

(Sanhedrin, 91a—91b.)

V

SELECTIONS FROM THE ZOHAR.

I, 19b. THE SYMBOL OF THE NUT.

King Solomon, when he " descended into the nut garden " (*S.S* VI, 11), took a nut-shell (*klifah*) and drew an analogy from its layers to those spirits which inspire sensual desires in human beings, as it is written, " and the delights of the sons of men are from male and female demons " (Eccl. II, 8). . . . The Holy One, blessed be He, found it necessary to create all these things in the world to ensure its permanency, so that there should be, as it were, a brain with many membranes encircling it. The whole world is constructed on this principle, upper and lower, from the first mystic point up to the furthest removed of all the stages. They are all coverings to one another, brain within brain and spirit within spirit, so that one is a shell to another. The primal point is an innermost light of a translucency, tenuity, and purity passing comprehension. The extension of that point becomes a " palace " (*Hekal*), which forms a vestment for that point with a radiance which is still unknowable on account of its translucency. The " palace " which is a vestment for that unknowable point is also a radiance which cannot be comprehended, yet withal less subtle and translucent than the primal mystic point. This " palace " extends into the primal light, which is a vestment for it. From this point there is extension after extension, each one forming a vestment to the other, being in the relation of membrane and brain to one another. Although at first a vestment, each one becomes a brain to the next stage. The same process takes place below, so that on this model man in this world combines brain and shell, spirit and body, all for the better ordering of the world. When the moon was in connection with the sun she was luminous, but as soon as she separated from the sun and was assigned the charge of her own hosts, she reduced her status and her light, and shells upon shells were created for covering the brain, and all for the benefit of the brain. Hence *meoroth* is written defectively. All this was for the benefit of the world, and hence it is written, " to give light upon the earth ".

I, 141–142a. THE WELLS OF ISAAC.

" And thou shalt be like a watered garden " (Isaiah, LVIII, 11): that is, like the celestial garden, whose waters never fail, but flow on for ever and ever. " And like a spring of waters whose waters fail not " (*ib*.): alluding to the river that issues from Eden and flows on for all eternity, Observe that the " well of living waters " is a symbol within a symbol for guiding faith. There is the well which is the very source of the waters, and there is the well which is fed by that source of water. There are thus two grades, which are, however, really one with two aspects, male and female in fitting union. The well and the issue of waters are one, designated by the name of " well ", it being at once the supernal never-ceasing fountain and the well that is filled by it. And whoever gazes at that well gazes at the true object of faith. This is the symbol which the patriarchs transmitted in digging the well, in such a way as to indicate that the source and the well are indissoluble.

II, 15a. THE POWER OF THE RIGHTEOUS.

Then R. Simeon sat and listened while his son R. Eleazar stood and expounded mysteries of wisdom. And as he spoke his countenance was lit by the radiance of the sun, and his words ascended to the starry heights and flitted across the firmament. They thus continued for a space of two days, neither eating nor drinking and noticing neither day nor night. When they came forth they found that they had not tasted anything for two days. Said R. Simeon : " We are told that Moses was there with the Lord forty days and forty nights ; he did neither eat bread nor drink water (Ex. XXIV, 28). If we, who but for a brief space were caught up into that rapture of Divine contemplation, forgot to eat and drink, how much more so Moses ! "

When R. Hiya appeared before R. Judah the Saint and related this occurrence to him, R. Simeon b. Gamaliel, R. Judah's father, said : " R. Simeon b. Yohai is indeed a lion and his son likewise. He is different from all others of his kind. Of him it is written : " The lion hath roared, who will not fear " (Amos, III, 8). And if even the upper worlds do tremble before him, how much more then we ? A man who has no need of fasting to proclaim his desires to the Almighty, and to have them fulfilled, since he decides and the Holy One, blessed be He, confirms the decision ; or the Holy One deciding, he revokes the decision and it is annulled. As it is said : " There shall be one that ruleth over man, a righteous one ruling in the fear of the Lord " (2 Sam. XXIII, 3). The Holy One rules over man, but who rules over the Holy One ? Surely, the Righteous. For it may even be from time to time that the Holy One proposes and the Righteous disposes."

R. Judah said : " The Holy One, blessed be He, delights more in the prayer of the righteous than in any other thing soever ; yet, though it please Him better than all else, He does not always grant their requests, nor do all that they ask. He sometimes refuses to fulfil their wish."

II, 85b. GOD AND THE COMMANDMENTS.

We have been taught that when the " I " was proclaimed all those commandments of the Torah which are united in the " Body " of the Supernal Holy King were comprised in it ; for, indeed, all the commandments have their unifying centre in the " Body " of the King, some in the " Head ", some in the " Trunk ", some in the " Hands " and some in the " Feet ", and none of them ever step out and become separate from the " Body " of the King or lose connection with it. He, therefore, who transgresses against even one of the commandments of the Torah is as though he transgressed against the " Body " of the King, as it is written : " And they shall go forth and look upon the carcases of the men that have transgressed against me " (Isa. LXVI, 24)—as it were, against My very self. Woe unto the sinners who break the words of the Torah—they know not what they do.

II, 97a. THE PALACE OF LOVE.

This is a secret entrusted to the keeping of the wise alone, aud here is the substance thereof. In the midst of a mighty rock, a most recondite firmament, there is set a Palace which is called the Palace of Love. This is the region wherein the treasures of the King are stored, and all His love-kisses are there. All souls beloved of the Holy One enter into that Palace. And when the King Himself appears, " Jacob kisses Rachel " (Gen. XXIX, 11), that is, the Lord discovers each holy soul, and takes each in turn up to Himself, fondling and caressing her, " acting towards her after the manner of daughters ", even as a father treats his beloved daughter, fondling and caressing her and giving her presents. " Ear hath not heard nor eye seen . . . what he doeth to him who waiteth for him " (Isa. LXIV, 3) : as that daughter, the soul, has done her work in this world, so will the Holy One " do " His work on her in the world to come.

II, 156b. The Nourishment of the Soul.

Man's table enables him to attain to the delight of that other table : " he eats always at the king's table " (2 Sam. IX, 13), and as King David said, " Thou preparest a table before me " (Ps. XXIII, 4), which refers to the preparation of the Table in the other world for those from below ; for this is the joy and delight of the soul in the world to come. But is there a table set for the souls in the world to come ? Verily there is. In that world they eat of such food and with such satisfaction as the angels enjoy. And do the angels eat ? Verily they do. Such as theirs was the food upon which the Israelites were fed in the wilderness. This food is symbolical of the Dew which emanates from above, from the mystery of the world to come. It is the food of the light of the oil of holy anointing ; from it the righteous in the Garden of Eden derive their sustenance and are replete with joy. For in the Garden of Eden which is below the souls of the righteous put on a form which is like unto that which they had worn in this world ; but on Sabbaths and holydays they put off this form like a garment and ascend to those heavenly regions where they may behold the Lord in his glory and where they may fully enjoy the supernal delights.

II, 212a. Sufferings of the Messiah.

The Messiah, on his part, enters a certain Hall in the Garden of Eden, called the Hall of the Afflicted. There he calls for all the diseases and pains and sufferings of Israel, bidding them settle on himself, which they do. And were it not that he thus eases the burden from Israel, taking it on himself, no one could endure the sufferings meted out to Israel on account of their neglect of the Torah. So Scripture says, "Surely our diseases did he bear," etc. (Isa. LIII, 4). . . . For indeed, beyond number are the chastisements awaiting every man daily for the neglect of the Torah, all of which descended into the world at the time when the Torah was given. As long as Israel were in the Holy Land, by means of the Temple service and sacrifices they averted all evil diseases and afflictions from the world. Now it is the Messiah who is the means of averting them from mankind until the time when a man quits this world and receives his punishment.

II, 222a. THE SYMBOLISM OF THE TABERNACLE.

R. Judah cited the verse : " Beautiful bowery, the joy of the whole earth " (Ps. XLVIII, 3). " Observe," he said, " that when the Holy One, blessed be He, was about to create the world, He detached one precious stone from underneath His Throne of Glory and plunged it into the Abyss, one end of it remaining fastened therein while the other end stood out above ; and this other and superior head constituted the nucleus of the world, the point out of which the world started, spreading itself to right and left and into all directions, and by which it is sustained. That nucleus, that stone is called *shtiyah* (foundation), as it was the starting-point of the world. The name *shtiyah*, furthermore, is a compound of *shath* (founded) and *Yah* (God), signifying that the Holy One, blessed be He, made it the foundation and starting point of the world and all that is therein. Now the earth's expansion round the central point was completed in three concentric rings, each of a different hue and texture. The first ring, the nearest to the Point, is of the purest and most refined earth-material ; the second expansion, surrounding the first, is of a less polished, less refined earth-material than the first, but it is superior to the one surrounding it ; the third expansion consists of the darkest and coarsest earth-material of all. Then, surrounding that expansion, come the waters of the ocean that surrounds the whole world. Thus the point is in the centre and the various expansions encircle it. The first expansion embraces the Sanctuary and all its courts and enclosures and all its appurtenances, as well as the whole city of Jerusalem bounded by the wall ; the second expansion embraces the whole of the Land of Israel, the land which was declared holy ; the third expansion comprehends the rest of the earth, the dwelling-place of all the other nations. Then comes the great ocean which surrounds the whole. The whole arrangement is symbolised by the structure of the human eye. For just as in the human eye there are three concentric layers surrounding a central point, which forms the focus of vision, so is the world's vision focused in the central point, consisting of the Holy of Holies and the Ark and the Mercy Seat. Hence the description: "a beautiful bowery, the joy of the whole earth"

III, 57b. NEGLECT OF THE TORAH.

R. Simeon said : " I am amazed to see how little men pay heed to the will of their Master, and how they allow themselves to be wrapt in sleep until the day comes which will cover them with darkness, and when their Master will demand reckoning from them. The Torah calls aloud to them, but none inclines his ear. Mark now that in future generations the Torah will be forgotten and there will be none to close and open. Alas for that generation. There will be no generation like the present until the Messiah comes and knowledge shall be diffused throughout the world."

III, 166b. R. SIMEON'S REVELATION.

R. Simeon began : " A lovely hind and a graceful doe, let her breasts satisfy thee at all times " (Prov. V, 19). Torah, Torah, light of all worlds, how many seas, streams, sources and fountains spread before thee on all sides ! All are based on thee, upper and lower. The upper light goes forth from thee. Torah, Torah, what shall I say of thee, lovely hind and graceful doe, both in the upper and lower sphere ? Of those who love thee who is worthy to receive fitly thy nourishment ? Torah, Torah, cherished plaything of thy Master, who can disclose and reveal thy riddle and secret ? "
(After R. Simeon had said this) he wept, bowed his head between his knees, and kissed the earth. He saw a number of companions surrounding him. They said : " Tremble not, son of Yochai, fear not, holy lamp, write and rejoice in the joy of thy Master." So he wrote on that night all the words that he had heard, studied them, and recited them without forgetting one. That light streamed from him the whole night till daybreak. When the day broke he lifted up his eyes and saw a light in the sky. He lowered his eyes, raised them again, and saw a light overspreading the whole sky, and discerned in it a house of many colours. Rapture seized R. Simeon, but in that moment the light hid itself again. Meanwhile two messengers had come before him. They found him with his head between

his knees, and addressed him saying: "Peace to our Master, peace to him to whom upper and lower beings are fain to give greeting. Rise." R. Simeon raised himself and rejoiced to see them. They said to him: "Sawest thou not a breath of the spirit which the Lord has prepared for thee? Sawest thou not the reflexion of a house in the sky?" "I did." [Then they said to him: "In this house the Abyss has sent up a sanctuary which the Holiest has carried forth into the great sea. Its reflexion shone in the heaven." They further said to him: "Master, the (' heavenly ') Academy seeks thy greeting, and know that we have been sent to thee." Many old lessons of the Torah were re-learnt on that night. R. Simeon said to the messengers: "I beg of you to give some discourse of Torah." They replied: "We have not received permission. It is for this that we have come to thee, that the new lesson this time may come from thee."

VI

CHASSIDISM

(From Newman: Hasidic Anthology).

THE GOODNESS OF LIFE.

Said Rabbi Bunam: "Life is good, for it may bring to a man the joys of the World-to-Come. Hence if one shows contempt for life by self-destruction, he is deprived of his share of the World-to-Come." (p. 4)

THE CONTROL OF WRATH.

The Koretzer said: "Long ago I conquered my anger and placed it in my pocket. When I have need of it, I take it out." (p. 10)

THE BRATZLAVER ON ANGER.

Break your anger by compassion for the one with whom you are angry.

Anger and cruelty arise from a deficiency of understanding. Study the Torah to improve your understanding.

He who is obsessed by anger loses his image of God.

Anger prevents God's abundance from descending to us. (p. 11)

EVERY HUMAN TRAIT.

Said the Besht: " Man should learn pride, and not be proud; he should learn anger, but not feel angry.   For man should be a complete personality, possessing all human traits.   Does not the Torah picture God as possessing both justice and mercy." (p. 31)

THREE TYPES OF CHARACTER.

Said the Yud[1]: " There are three types of character among servants of God.   The servant of the Lord who labours the entire day and yet believes he has as yet accomplished nothing stands at the summit of merit.

The servant who has done nothing worth while in his service unto the Lord, and is aware of this, is a character of average merit.   He may yet commence to labour in the service of the Lord.

The servant who is a Zaddik and is proud of this knowledge is the least commendable character.   He deceives himself all his days, and his devotion to the Torah and the Mizwoth is wasted." (p. 32)

MELANCHOLY.

A Hasid bemoaned to the Lubliner that evil lusts plagued him and made him melancholy.   The Master said to him: " Above all sins rid yourself of melancholy, for it is more pernicious than sin.   When the Evil One rouses men to lust it is not his aim to make them sin, but to draw them through sin into the pit of melancholy."

Sadness is not a sin, but no sin hardens the heart so much as sadness.   Sadness is the worst quality in a man.   It is the attribute of an incurable egotist.   He is always thinking: Something should rightfully come to me; something is wrongfully lacking to me.   Whether in relation to Substance or Spirit, it is always " I ".   (pp. 242, 243)

PRAYER.

TARDY PRAYERS.

The Riziner was once asked why so many Zaddikim are heedless of the hours of prayer fixed by tradition.   He answered with a parable.   The King has appointed an hour for all who come upon their own business and after this hour they are barred from

[1] The same is said of the Great Maggid.

his presence. But those who come, not upon their own private affairs, but on matters of the common welfare, require no special hours; they are welcome at any time. (p. 329)

The Tzanzer was asked by a Hasid: What does the Rabbi do before praying? "I pray," was the reply, "that I may be able to pray properly". (p. 332)

OILING THE WHEELS WITH PRAYER.

The Berditschever saw a teamster dressed in Tallith and Tephillin lubricating the wheels of his wagon. The Rabbi exclaimed: "O Lord, what a holy people is Thine! Even when they oil the wheels of their wagons they pray unto Thee in Tallith and Tephillin!" (p. 333)

THE SABBATH.

Said the Medzibozer: "The Sabbath is greater than the World-to-Come, since the future world takes its source from the Sabbath and is thus merely a branch of it." (p. 408)

THE CHIEF PURPOSE.

The Gerer Rabbi said: "The Talmud (Sabbath 73) enumerates thirty-nine different kinds of work necessary for the construction of the Tabernacle. All these forms of labour had one supreme object—the Tabernacle."

In our various activities during the weekdays we should likewise emphasize the one chief purpose, namely the duty to honour the Sabbath. Then our every action will become sacred." (p. 404)

THE BRATZLAVER ON CHARITY.

Upon charity the universe is founded.

Through charity you may subdue the body to the soul, and folly to reason. Thus you will go forth from darkness to light, from death to life; from animality to humanity. You will lose forgetfulness and gain memory.

Charity has the weight of all Mizwoth together. (p. 40)

MONEY AND ITS USE.

The Rimanower Rabbi dreamed that he ascended to Heaven and heard an angel pleading with the Lord to grant Israel wealth, saying: " Behold how pious they are in poverty; vouchsafe unto them riches, and they will be many times as pious."

The Rabbi inquired the name of the angel. The reply was: He is called the Satan.

The Rabbi then exclaimed: " Leave us in poverty, O Lord. Safeguard us from the favours of the Satan." (p. 274)

TRUTH AND FALSEHOOD.

Said R. Bunam: " The Lord selected truth as his seal (Sabbath 55) because any other virtue may be a clever imitation of the true form, whereas any imitation of the truth is falsehood." (p. 487)

THE BRATZLAVER ON TRUTH AND FALSEHOOD.

The breath of a lie creates the Satan. (p. 488)

Falsehood corrupts the blood; truth purifies it. (p. 488)

Falsehoods are many, but truth is one. In the Unity of truth there is strength; truth is divine and it will surely triumph. (p. 488)

Where there is no truth, there is no peace. (p. 489)

THE MEZERITZER ON THOUGHT AND WISDOM.

Wisdom is God's garment.

Wisdom constantly receives influence from above and gives out spirituality below.

Thought is a world of freedom.

Oftentimes when you elevate a man's thoughts to God you may transform them." (pp. 475–476)

LEARNING FROM THE CHILD.

Rabbi Bunam said: " We may learn three things from the Child in serving the Lord. First, the child is always happy at being alive. Second, the child is always active. Third, the child always cries for anything he wishes. In the same fashion we should serve the Lord in a joyful mood; we should always be zealous to perform the Lord's commands; we should tearfully implore the Lord to fulfil our aspirations." (p. 42)

Learning From The Thief.

Rabbi Bunam said : " We may learn three things from a thief. First, he is not lazy to be active in his work in the middle of the night. Second, if he does not succeed on his first attempt, he repeats the endeavour several times until he has accomplished his goal. Third, he does not despise any article."

The man who wishes to serve the Lord aright should utilise the same methods. (p. 155)

The White Horse.

A young man came to the Riziner and asked to be ordained as a Rav. The Riziner enquired regarding his daily conduct, and the candidate replied : " I always dress in white ; I drink only water ; I place tacks in my shoes for self-mortification ; I roll naked in the snow ; and I order the Synagogue caretaker to give me forty stripes daily on my bare back."

Just then a white horse entered the courtyard, drank water, and began rolling in the snow. " I observe," said the Riziner, " this creature is white ; it drinks only water ; it has nails in its shoes ; it rolls in the snow, and receives more than forty stripes a day. Still it is nothing but a horse ! " (p. 17)

The Bird's Nest.

The Besht narrated this parable. A migrating bird of rare beauty flew past the royal palace and alighted on the top of a high palm tree. The King yearned to possess this beautiful creature and instructed his courtiers to form a human ladder, one to stand on the shoulders of the other, until the highest could throw a net upon the bird. Though only men of strength were chosen, one weakened, and the entire human structure collapsed to the ground. By virtue of one man's fault, the King's desire could not be fulfilled.

It is the same with us. The man of holiness depends upon the support of a lesser man, and the latter depends upon men of even lowlier quality in order to attain the summit of holiness and to bring down God's love. But when one person weakens, the whole structure totters and falls, and the Zaddik must begin anew. (p. 247)

The Measure of Suffering.

Boundless was the Apter's love for Israel. Once he broke into great lamentation and wept almost a half day without cease.

On this day Rabbi Sussya of Anipol visited Apt and came directly to Rabbi Abraham Joshua. " What is the cause of your weeping ? " he asked the Apter in his compelling fashion. " Has not the Holy Baal Shem commanded us to be always gay and cheerful ? "

The Apter cast a mournful glance at his friend and cried : " Sussya, Sussya, what will befall you ? Do you not feel the dreadful suffering and the bitter persecutions to which the people of Israel are subjected ? "

" I feel them," answered Rabbi Sussya, " but it is written in the Book of Zohar that God inflicts upon mankind only as much suffering as it can endure." (p. 484)

VOLUNTARY GALUTH.

Said the Komarner : " He who voluntarily leaves his home and wanders about as a beggar, living a life of discomfort, but trusting always in the Lord, becomes a partner in the ' Exile of the Shekinah '. His sins are forgiven and he understands the secrets of the Torah. Happy is the lot of those who go into ' exile ' ". (p. 502)

SONG WITHOUT WORDS.

The Ladier noticed an old man among his listeners who obviously did not comprehend the meaning of his discourse. He summoned him to his side and said : " I perceive that my sermon is unclear to you. Listen to this melody[1] and it will teach you how to cleave unto the Lord." The Ladier began to sing a song without words. It was a song of Torah, of trust in God, of longing for the Lord, and of love for Him.

" I understand now what you wish to teach " exclaimed the old man. " I feel an intense longing to be united with the Lord ". The Rabbi's melody became part of his every discourse henceforth, though it had no words. (p. 283)

[1] *V. p.* 142.

BIBLIOGRAPHY

This Bibliography contains books and essays useful for the study of Jewish Mysticism, but contains neither the original literature nor works on non-Jewish Mysticism, for which see Chapter IX.

For a more comprehensive bibliography see SHOLEM, "Bibliographia Kabbalistica" and "Major Trends of Jewish Mysticism".

Complete Translations.

The Babylonian Talmud : English Translation by J. EPSTEIN. German Translation by Laz. GOLDSCHMIDT.

The Midrashim : English Translation by Maur. SIMON. German Translation by WINTER and WÜNSCHE.

The Zohar : English Translation by HARRY SPERLING and MAURICE SIMON. French Translation by JEAN DE PAULY.

Works on Jewish Mysticism.

ABELSON, J., *Jewish Mysticism.* London, 1913.

AHRENS, W. Ch., *Hebräische Amulette mit magischen Zahlenquadraten.* (In : Ost und West.) Berlin, 1916.

APTOWITZER, V., בית המקדש של מעלה (In : Tarbiz II.) Jerusalem, 1931.

BAECK, Leo, *Zum ' Sepher Jezira '.* (In : Monatschrift für Geschichte und Wissenschaft des Judentums, vol. 70.) Berlin, 1926.

   „ *Die zehn Sephiroth im Sepher Jezira.* (*Ibid.*, vol. 78.) 1934.

BAEHR, C. Chr. Wilh. Fel., *Symbolik des mosaischen Cultus*, 2nd ed. Heidelberg, 1874.

BEER, Peter, *Geschichte, Lehren und Meinungen aller bestandenen und noch bestehenden religiösen Sekten der Juden und der Geheimlehre oder Kabbalah.* 2 voll., Brünn, 1822.

BENAMOZEGH, Elia, *Israel et l'humanité. Étude sur le problème de la religion universelle et sa solution.* Paris, 1914.

BENDAVID, Lazarus, *Über den Glauben der Juden an einen künftigen Messias.* (In : Zeitschrift für die Wissenschaft des Judentums.) Berlin, 1822.

BENSION, Ariel, *The Zohar in Moslem and Christian Spain.* London, 1932.

BERGMANN, Hugo, *Die Heiligung des Namens.* (In : Vom Judentum.) Leipzig, 1914.

BIRNBAUM, Salomon, *Leben und Werke des Balschemm.* Berlin, 1920.

BLAU, Ludwig, *Das altjüdische Zauberwesen.* (In : Jahresberichte der Landes-Rabbinerschule in Budapest, 1897–8.)

BLOCH, Chajim, *Die Gemeinde der Chassidim.* Berlin-Wien, 1920.

„ *Israel der Gotteskämpfer.* Berlin-Wien, 1920.

„ *Kabbalistische Sagen.* Leipzig, 1925.

BLOCH, Philipp, *Geschichte der Entwicklung der Kabbala und der jüdischen Religionsphilosophie.* (In : Winter und Wünsche, Die jüdische Literatur seit Abschluss des Kanons, III.) Trier, 1894.

„ *Die Kabbalah auf ihrem Höhepunkt und ihre Meister.* Pressburg, 1905.

„ *Die* יורדי מרכבה, *die Mystiker der Gaonenzeit und ihr Einfluss auf die Liturgie.* (In : Monatsschrift für die Geschichte und Wissenschaft des Judentums, vol. 37.) Breslau, 1893.

BOCK, Emil, *Das Alte Testament und die Geistesgeschichte der Menschheit.* Stuttgart, 1934–6.

BRECHER, Gideon, *Das Transcendentale, Magic und magische Heilarten im Talmud.* Wien, 1850.

BREHIER, *Les idées philosophiques et religieuses de Philon d'Alexandrie.* Paris, 1908.

BUBER, Martin, *Jewish Mysticism and the Legends of Baalshem,* transl. by Lucy Cohn. London, 1931.

„ *Die Geschichten des Rabbi Nachman.* Frankfurt a.M., 1906.

„ *Die Legende des Baalschem.* Frankfurt a.M., 1908.

„ *Der grosse Maggid und seine Nachfolge.* Frankfurt a.M, 1922.

„ *Das verborgene Licht.* Frankfurt a.M., 1924.

„ *Mein Weg zum Chassidismus.* Frankfurt a.M., s.a.

CASTELLI, David, *Gli antecedenti della Cabbala nella Bibbia e nella letteratura talmudica.* (In : Actes du 12me Congrès des Orientalistes 1899, vol. III.) Turin, 1903.

DAICHES, Samuel, *Babylonian Magic in the Talmud and in the Late Jewish Literature.* (Publ. of the Jews' College No. 5.) London, 1913.

DODS, Marcus, *Forerunners of Dante.* Edinburgh, 1903.

DORNSEIFF, Franz, *Das Alphabet in Mystik und Magie.* Leipzig, 1922.

DUBNOW, Simon, תולדות החסידות. Tel Aviv, 1930–31.

EHRENPREIS, Marcus, *Die Entwicklung der Emanationslehre in der Kabbala des XIII. Jahrhunderts.* Frankfurt a.M., 1895.

ENCAUSSE, Gerard (pseud. Papus), *La Kabbale, tradition secrète de l'occident.* Paris, 1892.

EPSTEIN, Abraham, ספר יצירה. (In: Beiträge zur hebräischen Altertumskunde.) Wien, 1887.

FISCHER, Oskar, *Der Ursprung des hebräischen Alphabets.* Leipzig, 1917.

„ *Orientalische und griechische Zahlensymbolik.* Leipzig, 1918.

FRANCK, Adolphe, *La Kabbala ou la philosophie des Hebreux.* Paris, 1843. (2nd ed. 1889. 3rd ed. 1892. German Transl. by Ad. Jellinek.)

FREUDENTHAL, J., *Spinoza, sein Leben und seine Lehre.* Stuttgart, 1904.

FRIEDLANDER, Moritz, *Der vorchristliche jüdische Gnosticismus.* Göttingen, 1898.

„ *Die religiösen Bewegungen innerhalb des Judentums im Zeitalter Jesu.* Berlin, 1905.

FULLER, J. F. C., *The Secret Wisdom of the Qabalah.* London, 1937.

GASTER, Moses, *The Origin of the Kabbala.* (Judith Montefiore College, Ramsgate, Report for 1893–4.)

„ *Das Schiur Komah.* (In: Monatsschrift für Geschichte und Wissenschaft des Judentums, vol. 37.)

„ *The Sword of Moses, an Ancient Book of Magic.* London, 1896.

GELBHAUS, S., *Die Metaphysik der Ethik Spinozas im Quellenlichte der Kabbalah.* Wien-Brünn, 1917.

GINSBURG, Christian D., *The Essenes, their History and Doctrines.* London, 1864.

„ *The Kabbalah, its Doctrines, Development and Literature.* London, 1865.

GINZBERG, Lewis, *The Legends of the Jews.* 6 voll. New York, 1909–28.

GINZBURG, S., *The Life and Works of Moses Hayyim Luzzatto.* Philadelphia, 1931.

GOLDBERG, Oskar, *Die Wirklichkeit der Hebräer. Einleitung in das System des Pentateuch,* vol. 1. Berlin, 1925.

GOLDSCHMIDT, Lazarus, ספר יצירה *Das Buch der Schöpfung.* (Hebrew and German.) Frankfurt a.M., 1898.

bin GORION, M. J. (Berdyczewski), *Die Sagen der Juden.* 5 voll. Frankfurt a.M., 1913–27.

„ *Kabbalistische Geschichten (Der Born Judas,* vol. 6.) Leipzig, s.a.

GRÄTZ, H., *Gnosticismus und Judentum.* Krotoschin, 1846.

„ *Frank und die Frankisten.* Breslau, 1868.

„ *Die mystische Literatur in der gaonäischen Epoche.* (In: Monatsschrift für Geschichte und Wissenschaft des Judentums VIII, 1859.)

GRETHER, Oscar, *Name und Wort Gottes im Alten Testament*. (Beiheft zur Zeitschrift für alttestamentliche Wissenschaft 64). Giessen, 1934.

HASENCLEVER, Richard, *Die Grundzüge der esoterischen Harmonik des Altertums, im Anschluss an Albert . . . v. Thimus*. Cologne, 1870.

HELD, Hans Ludwig, *Das Gespenst des Golem*. München, 1927.

HERTZ, J. H., *Mystic Currents in Ancient Israel. Rise and Development of Cabala*. (Sermons, Addresses and Studies III.) London, 1938.

„ *On Cabala.* (In : *Hibbert's Journal*, July, 1912.)

HORODEZKY, Samuel Abba, *Rabbi Nachman von Brazlow. Beitrag zur Geschichte der jüdischen Mystik*. Berlin, 1910.

„ *Mystisch-religiöse Strömungen unter den Juden in Polen im 16. bis 18. Jahrhundert*. Leipzig, 1914.

„ *Religiöse Strömungen mit besonderer Berücksichtigung des Chassidismus*. Bern-Leipzig, 1920.

‎החסידים והחסידות. Berlin-Jerusalem, 1922.

JAARI, Abraham, ‎אגרות ארץ ישראל. Tel Aviv, 1943.

JACOB, B., *Der Pentateuch*. Leipzig, 1905.

JELLINEK, Adolf, *Moses ben Schemtob da Levn und sein Verhältnis zum Sohar*. Leipzig, 1857.

„ *Beiträge zur Geschichte der Kabbala*, I. und II. Heft. Leipzig, 1852.

„ *Auswahl kabbalistischer Mystik* I. Leipzig, 1853.

„ *Philosophie und Kabbala*. I. containing : Abr. Abulafia's Sendschreiben über Philosophie und Kabbala. Leipzig, 1854.

„ *Der Mensch als Ebenbild Gottes, von Sabbatai Donolo*. Leipzig, 1854.

„ *Bet ha-Midrasch. Sammlung kleiner Midraschim*. Leipzig, 1853–71.

„ *Apokalypse des Pseudo-Propheten und Pseudo-Messias Abr. Abulafia*. (In : Jubelschrift Grätz.) Breslau, 1887.

JOEL, D. H., *Die Religionsphilosophie des Sohar und ihr Verhältnis zur allgemeinen jüdischen Theologie; zugleich eine kritische Beleuchtung der Franck'schen 'Kabbala'*. Leipzig, 1849.

KAHANE, David, ‎והחסידים. תזלות המקבלים השבתאים. Tel Aviv, 1927.

KARPPE, S., *Etudes sur les origines et la nature du Zohar*. Paris, 1901.

KASTEIN, Joseph, *Sabbatai Zewi*, London, 1931.

KEFERSTEIN, Frieda, *Philos Lehre von den göttlichen Mittelwesen*. Leipzig, 1846.

KING, C. W., *The Gnostics and Their Remains*. London, 1887.

KLEUKER, Joh. Fr., *Über Natur und Ursprung der Emanationslehre bei den Kabbalisten*. Riga, 1786.

KOHUT, Alexander, *Über die jüdische Angelologie und Dämonologie in ihrer Abhängigkeit vom Parsismus*. Leipzig, 1866.

KRISTIANPOLLER, Alexander, *Traum und Traumdeutung*. (In : Monumenta Hebraica. Monumenta Talmudica.) Wien-Berlin, 1923.

KUNITZ, Moses, בר יוחאי. Budapest-Wien, 1815.

LANDAUER, M. H., *Jehova und Elohim oder die althebräische Gotteslehre als Grundlage der Geschichte der Symbolik und der Gesetzgebung der Bücher Mosis*. Stuttgart-Tübingen, 1838.

„   *Wesen und Form des Pentateuchs*. Stuttgart-Tübingen, 1838.

„   *Vorläufiger Bericht über mein Studium der Münchner hebräischen Handschriften in Ansehung des Sohar*. (In : Literaturblatt des Orients, 6. Jahrgang, 1845.)

LANGER, Jiři, Devět bran (*Nine Gates ; Czech.*) Prague, 1937.

LEVERTOFF, Paul, *Die religiöse Denkweise der Chassidim, nach den Quellen dargestellt*. Leipzig, 1918.

LEVI, Eliphas, *Le Livre des splendeurs* . . . . . *Études sur les origines de la Kabbala*. 1. Idra sutta. Paris, 1894. 2nd ed. 1902.

LUCIUS, P. E., *Die Therapeuten und ihre Stellung in der Geschichte der Askese*. Strassburg, 1879.

„   *Der Essenismus in seinem Verhältnis zum Judentum*. Strassburg, 1881.

LUEKEN, Wilhelm, *Michael. Eine Darstellung und Vergleichung der jüdischen und der morgenländisch-christlichen Tradition vom Erzengel Michael*. Göttingen, 1898.

MARCUS, Ahron (pseud. Verus), *Der Chassidismus*. Pleschen, 1901.

MARMORSTEIN, Arthur, *The Old Rabbinic Doctrine of God*. London, 1927.

MEAD, G. R. S., *Fragments of a Faith Forgotten*. London, 1906.

MORDELL, Ph., *The Origin of Letters and Numbers according to the Sepher Yesirah*. (The Jewish Quarterly Review No. II, pp. 557–83, No. III, pp. 517–44.)

MATHERS, *The Kabbalah Unveiled*. London, 1887.

MEISL, Joseph, *Haskala*. Berlin, 1919.

MOLITOR, Franz Joseph, *Philosophie der Geschichte oder über die Tradition in dem alten Bunde und ihre Beziehung zur Kirche des neuen Bundes*. 4 parts. Mit vorzüglicher Rücksicht auf die Kabbala. Frankfurt a.M., 1827–55.

MÜLLER, Ernst, *Der Sohar und seine Lehre. Einführung in die Gedankenwelt der Kabbala*. 2nd ed. Wien, 1923.

MÜLLER, Ernst, *Der Sohar. Das heilige Buch der Kabbala,
Ausgewählte Texte.* Übersetzt von E. Müller. Wien,
1932.
„ *Abraham Ibn Esra. Das Buch der Einheit.* Übersetzt
und erläutert. Berlin, 1920.
„ עֵל סֵפֶר יְצִירָה. (In : Metsudah II.) London, 1943.
„ עֵל הַמְּסְתּוֹרִין בְּכִתְבֵי הַקֹּדֶשׁ. (*Ibid.*, III–IV.) London, 1945.
MYER, Isaac. *Qabbalah. The Philosophical Writings of Solomon
Ibn Gabirol or Avicebron and their connection with the
Hebrew Qabbalah and Sepher ha-Zohar.* Philadelphia,
1888.
NEWMAN, Louis I. Th., *Hasidic Anthology. Tales and Teachings
of the Hasidim.* In Collaboration with Sam. Spitz.
New York-London, 1934.
ODEBERG, *The 3 Book Enoch.* London, 1928.
OESTERLEY, Wilh. Osc. Emil, *A Fresh Approach to the Psalms.*
London, 1937.
PAPUS, pseud. see ENCAUSSE, Gerard.
PASCHER, Josef, *Der Königsweg zur Vergottung und Wiedergeburt
bei Philon von Alexandreia.* Berlin, 1931.
PAULY, Jean de, *Le Livre du Zohar.* (*Extraits.*) Paris, 1925.
PFLAUM, Heinz, *Leone Ebreo.* (Soncino Blotter S.A.) Berlin,
1930.
PISTIS SOPHIA. *A Gnostic Gospel.* Translated from the Latin
by G. R. S. Mead. London, 1891.
RIESSLER, Paul, *Altjüdisches Schrifttum ausserhalb der Bibel.*
Übersetzt und erläutert. Augsburg, 1928.
ST. YVES D'ALVEYDRE, Alexandre, *Mission des Juifs.* Paris,
1883.
SCHECHTER, Solomon, *Safed in the 16th Century.* (In : Studies
in Judaism, vol. 2.) London, 1896 sq.
SCHOLEM, Gerhard, *Bibliographia Kabbalistica.* Berlin, 1925.
„ *Article " Kabbala " in Encyclopædia Judaica.*
„ · *Zur Frage der Entstehung der Kabbala.* (In : Korrespondenz-
blatt des Vereins zur Erhaltung einer Akademie der
Wissenschaft des Judentums.) Berlin, 1928.
„ *Major Trends of Jewish Mysticism.* Jerusalem, 1941.
„ סֵפֶר הַזֹּהַר? פֶּם חַבֵּרִר מֹשֶׁה דִּי לִיאוֹן אֶת. (In : Madda,
ha-Yahadut I.) *Jerusalem*, 1926.
SCHULTZ, Wolfgang, *Dokumente der Gnosis.* Jena, 1910.
SCHÜRER, Emil, *The Jewish People in the Time of Jesus Christ.*
(Translated from the German.) Edinburgh, 1900.
SCHWAAB, Moise, *Vocabulaire de l'angelologie d'après les
manuscrits Hebreux de la Bibliothèque Nationale.* Paris,
1897.

SELIG, Gottfried, *Sepher Schimmusch Tchillim oder Gebrauch der Psalmen zum leiblichen Wohl der Menschen.* Stuttgart, 1853.

SILVER, Abba Hillel, *A History of Messianic Speculation in Israel from the 1st to the 17th Centuries.* New York, 1927.

STEINER, Rudolf, *Die Geheimnisse der biblischen Schöpfungsgeschichte.* (Zehn Vorträge 1910.) Dornach, 1932.

STENRING, *Book Jezira.* London, 1927.

STERN, Ignaz, *Versuch einer umständlichen Analyse des Sohar.* (In : Ben Chananja I-V.) Szegedin, 1858–62.

STÖSSEL, David, *Sal. ibn Gabirol als Philosoph und Förderer der Kabbala.* Leipzig, 1881.

TEITELBAUM, Mordechai, הרב מלאדי ומפלנת חב,ד. *I, II. Der Rabh von Ladi, sein Leben, Werk und System sowie die Geschichte der Sekte Chabad.* Warschau, 1910, 1913.

THIMUS, Albert von, *Die harmonikale Symbolik des Altertums.* 2 voll. Cologne, 1868–76. (Abridged Report by Richard Hasenclever, *ibid.,* 1870).

THOLUCK, Fr. Aug., *Wichtige Stellen des rabbinischen Buches Sohar in Text und mit Übersetzung.* 4th ed. Berlin, 1876.

VULLIAUD, Paul, *La Kabbale juive, histoire et doctrine.* Paris, 1923.

WAITE, *The Holy Kabbalah. A Study of the Secret Tradition in Israel.* London, 1929.

WEINSTEIN, N. J., *Zur Genesis der Agada. Beitrag zur Entstehung und Entwicklungsgeschichte des talmudischen Schrifttums. II. Die alexandrinische Agada.* Frankfurt a.M., 1901.

WESTCOTT, William Wynn, *Sepher Yetzirah. The Book of Formation.* Bath, 1887.

WIENER, Max, *Messias (Dichtung).* Wien-Leipzig, 1919.

„ *Die Lyrik der Kabbalah.* Wien-Leipzig, 1920.

WÜNSCHE, August, *Aus Israels Lehrhallen.* Leipzig, 1907.

ZEITLIN, Hilel, מפתח לספר הזהר. (In : Ha-Tekufa VI, VII, IX.) קדמות המסתורין בישראל. (*ibid.,* V.) 1920.

INDEX OF NAMES